Senses

Cross-Curriculum Units for Theme Teaching

Written by Patricia O'Brien

Edited by Nan Ryan

Illustrated by Darcy Tom

Teaching & Learning Company

1204 Buchanan St., P.O. Box 10
Carthage, IL 62321-0010

Hearing

Sight

Smell

Touch

Taste

Cover by Darcy Tom

Copyright © 1997, Teaching & Learning Company

ISBN No. 1-57310-076-5

Printing No. 987654321

Teaching & Learning Company
1204 Buchanan St., P.O. Box 10
Carthage, IL 62321-0010

This book belongs to

_____

Table of Contents

TLC10076 Copyright © Teaching & Learning Company, Carthage, IL 62321-0010

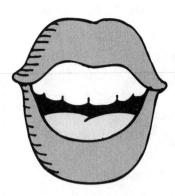

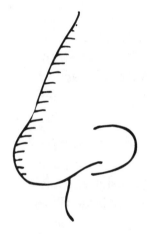

Dear Teacher or Parent,

This book of the five senses is designed to be used as a teacher resource and idea book for educators in the primary grades.

Each of us learns about the world around us through our senses, but children are especially open to new experiences. Through senses, their world is enlivened. They receive information through their eyes, ears, nose, tongue and skin. They see shapes and colors. They hear loud and quiet sounds. Children notice familiar smells and mysterious aromas. They investigate new and different tastes and savor their favorites. Children feel pain. They examine textures. As they become more aware of their surroundings, they can more easily cope with confusing concepts, find answers to puzzling questions, solve problems and better appreciate their environment.

In this book, each of the senses is introduced, discussed and related to personal experiences. Questions are asked to spark the imagination and to encourage critical and creative thinking. Literature selections are presented, investigated and enjoyed. Discovery Experiences provide occasions to challenge and delight. Suggested Activities that cross the curriculum present opportunities for the students to use their senses as they investigate the world around them. Books of fiction and non-fiction, listed in the bibliography, offer additional review material.

Literature Connections give students the opportunity to enjoy stories together, to share ideas and insights, to relate incidents to their own lives, to view situations from a different perspective and to confirm what they already know and believe. Each of the featured books focuses on one of the senses. Questions and activities have been designed to enrich the learning experience.

Discovery Experiences build on the natural curiosity of the child. A sense of wonder is captured as students think more deeply and examine things in a new way. They are encouraged to observe, measure, categorize and record a variety of related materials through investigation. While most students will not grow up to be scientists, their lives will be enriched because they have taken time to wonder, explore and discover.

Activities have been suggested that extend the lessons and connect classroom experiences with real-life situations. They are planned to provide for individual learning styles and interest and to furnish opportunities to share creatively.

Any successful program ultimately depends on teachers' abilities to communicate their enthusiasm and sense of wonder to their students.

Sincerely,

Pat

Patricia O'Brien

Sight

Nature Connection

Do You Know?

How do you see?

How are your eyes like a camera?

Why do bright lights make you squint?

Teacher Background

The eye is a wonderful sensory organ. But no matter how well all the parts work together, unless there is light, you cannot see. The iris is the colored part of the eye. It regulates the amount of light that enters the eye through the pupil. If the light is bright, the iris contracts, making the pupil smaller. When it is dark, the iris opens to let more light in.

The transparent lens, about the size of a pea, is located behind the iris. It changes shape so it can focus light rays on the retina at the back of the eye. The cornea covers and protects the lens. It also aids in focusing light. Muscles control the shape of the lens to allow it to focus on objects near and far away. Most of the space in the eye contains vitreous humor, a clear jelly-like substance that gives the eye its shape.

The retina is lined with light-sensitive rod and cone cells. Rod cells respond only to black and white and need only a little light. Cones let us see in color when there is bright light. When an image reaches the retina, it is upside down. The brain unscrambles the impulses it receives through the optic nerve and allows us to see things around us.

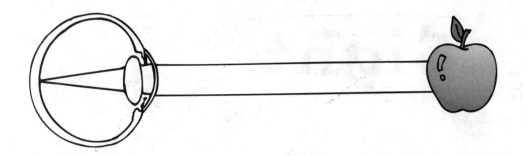

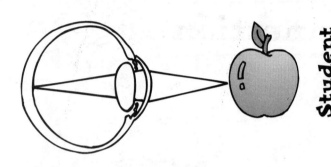

Information

You use sight more than any of your senses. You see the world surrounding you. You can compare colors, shapes and sizes. Because you have the sense of sight, you can learn a lot of things by reading and observing what is going on around you. You can use a computer, play ball and ride a bike. You are able to look out for cars when crossing the street, watch stars sparkling in the night sky and see your friends.

The main parts of the eye are the iris, pupil, lens, retina and optic nerve. Light enters the eye through the pupil, the dark part of the eye. The colored iris controls the amount of light that is admitted. Light passes through the lens and is focused on the retina at the back of the eye. From the retina the information travels along the optic nerve that connects the eye to the brain. There is no sight without light.

Your eyes usually can adjust to seeing things nearby and far away. Sometimes the lens cannot focus the rays of light on the retina because the shape of the eye is either too long or too short. When the rays come into focus in front of or behind the retina, the image will be blurred.

Glasses correct vision by bending the light so it will reach the retina at just the right place. Contact lenses work the same way, but the lens fits right over the eye.

Talk About

Name the most beautiful thing you have seen.

Words to Know

iris	lens	optic nerve	pupil	retina

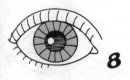

8   Sight

Discovery Experiences

☐ Reading Braille

Blind people depend more on their senses of hearing and touch than those who are sighted. They learn to read special books printed in Braille, using their fingers to feel the pattern of dots representing each letter.

Share with the children books printed in Braille. The public library should be a good resource. Reproduce page 21 for each child. Give the students the opportunity to experience reading with their fingers.

☐ Visual Memory

Visual memory can be improved. Students work in pairs to do the following activity.

Question: How well do you remember what you see?

Materials: construction paper, two pieces for each pair; a variety of small objects such as coins, toothpicks, buttons, shells, toys and crayons

Procedure: After the objects are arranged on one piece of paper by one person, the other person has 30 seconds to study the display. Cover the items with the other piece of paper and see how many he or she can remember seeing on the paper. Reverse roles and repeat.

Have the students talk about the methods they use for remembering. Do they pay attention to the colors or shapes of the objects? Do they look for patterns? After the students share techniques for remembering, have them try a new technique to see if it improves their memory.

To vary the procedure, allow less time to view the display, or add more items, one at a time.

☐ Seeing in 3-D

Question: Are two eyes better than one?

Procedure 1: Face a partner and cover one eye with your hand. Reach out with the index finger of the other hand. Touch your partner's finger in midair. Repeat using both eyes.

Procedure 2: Hold one pencil in each hand at arm's length. Using both eyes, touch the pencil points together. Try again with one eye closed. What happened?

Explanation: Because our eyes are spaced apart, we see objects from two slightly different angles. Our brain compares the two images and allows us to better judge distance. Using only one eye limits our ability to tell how far away an object is.

☐ The Changing Pupil

The next time the lights are turned off when you view a film or slides, notice how your eyes adapt to the dark.

Question: Why do you squint after the lights are turned on in a darkened room?

Explanation: In a darkened room, the pupil of the eye gets larger to allow in more light. When the lights come on, it takes a short while for the pupil to adjust.

☐ Light and Dark

Materials
mirrors

Directions

Observe both eyes, noting the size of the pupils. Go outside, if it is sunny, or into a brightly lit room. Cover one eye for about two minutes. After you uncover your eye, look in the mirror to compare the size of the pupils. What do you notice?

Explanation: It is easier to observe the pupil, but it is actually the iris that has opened to let more light into the covered eye and closed to protect the uncovered one.

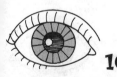

10   Sight

☐ Try This

Close one eye, extend an arm and point to something in the distance. While pointing at the object, look at it with your other eye. Can you explain what happened?

Explanation: Just as you are right-handed or left-handed, you are also right- or left-eyed. One eye is stronger (called dominant).

☐ Two Views = One

Materials
2 bathroom tissue tubes for each student

Directions

Procedure: Put one tube to each eye and look through both at the same time. Bring the tubes together so the two ends away from your eyes touch. What happened? Explain what you think occurred.

Explanation: Each eye views things at a slightly different angle. Your brain is able to put the two images together so you can see one picture.

☐ Optical Trick 1

Materials
each student will need one
3" x 5" (8 x 13 cm)
unlined card
glue
pencil with an eraser
felt-tipped markers or
crayons
ruler
tape

Procedure:

1. Use the ruler to measure a 2" x 4" (5 x 10 cm) rectangle. Cut out and fold in half.

2. Draw and color an animal on one half of the card.

3. On the other half, draw lines to make bars on a cage.

4. Tape the pencil to the card inside the fold. Tape the open ends closed. The picture should show on the front and back of the card, with the pencil inside.

5. Place the end of the pencil between the palms and roll quickly back and forth. The animal will appear to be in a cage.

Explanation: As the card rotates, two images are sent to the brain—the animal and the bars. The rapid rotation fools the eyes into thinking it is receiving one image and the animal appears to be in the cage.

☐ Optical Trick 2

Instruct the students to hold a tube to their right eye and focus on an object in the distance. Place their open left hand, with the palm facing them, halfway along the tube. Children should keep both eyes open. Do they notice anything unusual?

Explanation: Each eye sees independently. The brain combines the two images. The object in the distance seems to be seen through a hole in your hand.

☐ Optical Trick 3

Have the children touch their two index fingers together and hold them about 3" (8 cm) away from their eyes. Children should focus their eyes beyond their fingers. Now move the fingers slightly apart. Next, have them wiggle their fingers slowly up and down.

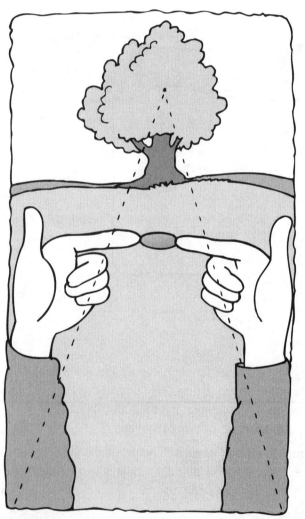

12 Sight

Suggested Activities

Pinhole Camera

Your eye works like a camera, but much better. Both need light to produce a picture. Both have a lens that centers the light. In a camera, the lens focuses the image on film, where light-sensitive chemicals record the picture. Before you can see the pictures taken by the camera, the film has to be developed. Your lens directs the image to the retina at the back of your eye. There, light-sensitive chemicals send nerve impulses to your brain where the picture is automatically processed.

The pinhole camera is the earliest type of camera. Below are directions for making and using the camera.

Materials
diagram (page 22)
aluminum foil
tracing paper
masking tape
craft knife
pencil
scissors
square tissue box

Directions

1. You will need an empty tissue box for each camera. Remove the clear plastic from the box opening.
2. Adults only! Use a craft knife to cut out the small square in the side opposite the opening in the box.
3. Tape along the edges to seal out any light.
4. Tape aluminum foil over the small square.
5. Make a small pinhole in the foil.
6. Tape tracing paper over the box opening.

To Use: Hold the camera with the pinhole facing away from you. Point it toward an object in bright light. The image will appear upside down on the tracing paper. To see a stronger image, follow the example of early photographers. Use a cloth to cover your head and the back of the box. Do you know why the image is upside down?

Explanation: Light from the top of the image travels downward through the pinhole and registers at the bottom of the tracing paper. The bottom of the image reflects light upward and appears at the top of the paper.

It is possible to produce a black and white photograph with a pinhole camera, but you would need photographic paper to replace the tracing paper a shutter for the pinhole and the use of a dark room and developing equipment.

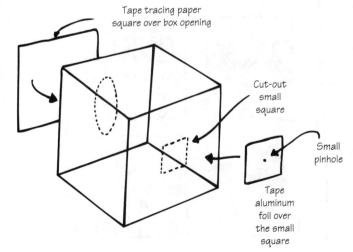

Tape tracing paper square over box opening

Cut-out small square

Small pinhole

Tape aluminum foil over the small square

Click

To give the children experience in taking photographs, purchase two or three one-time-use cameras. Give everyone a chance to snap a picture. Even if some of the prints don't come out, it can be a good learning experience. Next time they may approach the project differently.

1. Before taking photos, discuss basic picture-taking techniques. Talk about distance, light and shadows.

2. Let the children go outside to shoot their special pictures.

3. The children may talk about their snapshots after the pictures have been developed.

Story Starters

Share magazine photographs that could be used as story starters. Talk about what the pictures remind them of, what could have happened before they were taken and what might happen afterwards. Have each student select a photo to use as a story idea, imagining themselves in the situation suggested by the picture.

Snapshots Plus

Have the children take pictures while on a field trip or for a special occasion. They should be on the look out for shots that could be used as a story starter. Use the prints to promote ideas for original stories.

Publish the photos and stories in a class book or display them on the bulletin board.

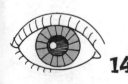

14   Sight

Shapes and Colors

Prepare rubber stamps for printing. Cut different sizes of circles, squares, rectangles and triangles from clean Styrofoam™ meat trays. Use tacky white glue to attach each shape to a pre-cut wood block or empty 35mm film canister. Allow four hours to dry.

Have the children make designs or realistic images using the stamps. They may add lines to their creations, use various sizes of one shape, mix the shapes and sizes and experiment with different colored ink pads. Remind them to wipe the stamp clean before using another color.

Cartoons

A cartoonist uses a few lines to show an expression that conveys surprise, boredom, anger, happiness or a number of other emotions. Share *Feelings*, by Aliki with the class. Several emotions are portrayed in story, verse and dialogue. The cartoon-like illustrations will provide inspiration for young artists.

1. Bring in several cartoons and comic strips to share with the class. How many different looking eyes can they find? Can they recognize the emotions shown?

2. Reproduce page 23 and have the class follow directions to become cartoonists.

3. Tell the students to feature two of the characters they created in a cartoon strip. They should decide on a setting or event and think about what the characters might say to each other.

Note: Write the dialogue before making the balloons.

Eye Color: A Bulletin Board Bar Graph

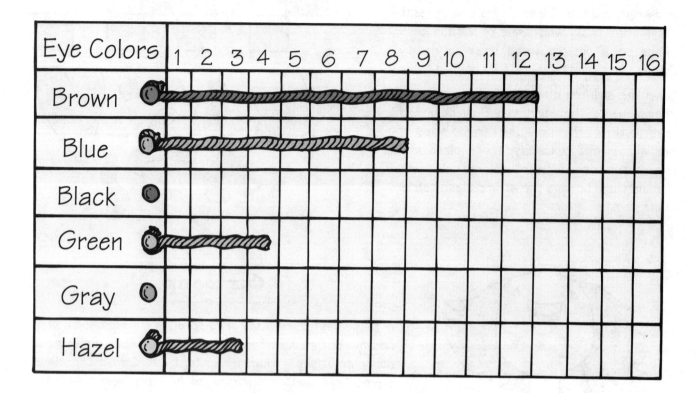

Eye Colors	1	2	3	4	5	6	7	8	9	10	11	12	13	14	15	16
Brown																
Blue																
Black																
Green																
Gray																
Hazel																

Eye color is inherited from your parents. The color of the iris has nothing to do with how well you see. People with light-colored eyes are more sensitive to bright lights.

Make a bar graph to show how many students share the same eye color. Tack heavy yarn or twine to the bulletin board to make the graph. Write eye colors (brown, blue, black, green, gray, hazel) on the vertical axis and numbers across the top or bottom.

Materials: 1½" (4 cm) squares of white paper, crayons, mirrors

Directions:

1. Students should work with a partner. Use crayons to try to match the color of their partner's iris on the square. Use the mirrors to check accuracy.

2. Place the squares in the appropriate spots on the graph.

3. After the squares are in place, discuss the graph and compare the data.

4. Instruct the students to write three questions about the information found there.

    Sample: How many more students have brown eyes than blue?

Knots on a Counting Rope, by Bill Martin, Jr., and John Archambault, illustrated by Ted Rand.

Summary

Boy-Strength-of-Blue-Horses grows up blind. His grandfather guides him to meet challenges without fear. The boy and his grandfather retell the story of his life. Each time the story is told, a knot is added to the counting rope. When the rope is filled with knots, the boy will know the story and will be able to tell it by himself.

Getting Ready

Have you ever faced a situation when you were afraid to try something at first, but things turned out fine?

Reading the Story

Read *Knots on a Counting Rope* aloud once to get a feel for the tale. Answer any questions the children may have. Respond to their reactions.

Thinking About the Story

Use the following questions to review the story and investigate the plot:

1. How did the boy get his name? How did your parents decide on your name?

2. When did you first realize the boy was blind?

3. What did he mean when he said there are many ways to see?

4. Was winning the race important to the boy?

5. What did he learn during the race? How did he feel when he finished?

6. What was the best gift the boy's grandfather gave him?

Activities   Reading Theater

1. Divide the students into pairs. Have the student's partner read the dialogue between the boy and his grandfather. Notice that the boy's part is always flush with the margin, while the grandfather's is indented.
2. Divide the group into two parts. Present the story as a choral reading.

Character Study: Boy-Strength-of-Blue-Horses

1. Do you know someone whose name means something special?
2. Besides strong, what other words could be used to describe the boy?
3. If you could meet the boy, what questions would you like to ask him?
4. Write a cinquain featuring Boy-Strength-of-Blue-Horses.

    Line 1: One word to name the subject

    Line 2: Two words to describe the subject

    Line 3: Three words ending in -ing or -ed that show action

    Line 4: Four words to tell how the subject feels

    Line 5: One word to rename the title

Cinquain example:

    Rainbow

    Strong, patient.

    Seeing, listening, learning.

    Courageous, shy, powerful, gentle.

    Special child.

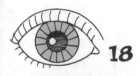

18   Sight

The Color Blue

1. Reread the part of the story where the grandfather told the boy about the color blue. Ask the students to think how they would explain a color to someone who has never seen color. Talk about ways it could be done. Focus on blue before thinking of other colors.

2. Enlarge the diagram at the top of page 24 on a chart. Fill in information found in the story and brainstorm to find additional ideas that would fit each category. How does blue taste? How does it smell? How does it feel and sound? Display the chart so that students can refer to it as they complete the assignment.

3. Use the words and phrases from the brainstorming session to write a sense poem about the color blue. Use the outline at the bottom of page 24 as a guide.

Colors

Each student should choose a color to describe. Distribute page 24, to be completed by everyone. Students with like colors may brainstorm; together; then use the ideas to write independently. Copy the poems onto another sheet of paper and illustrate.

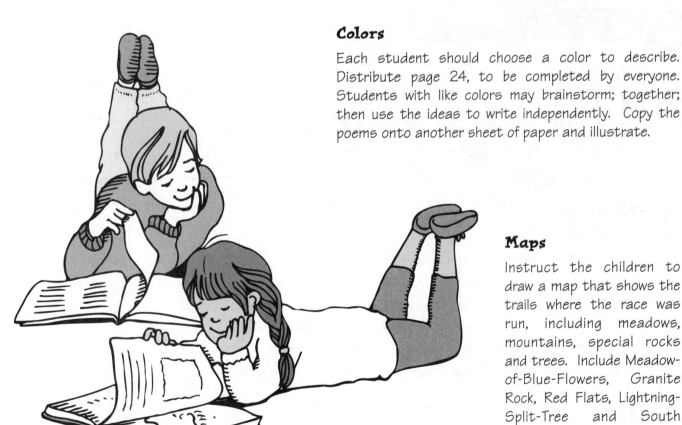

Maps

Instruct the children to draw a map that shows the trails where the race was run, including meadows, mountains, special rocks and trees. Include Meadow-of-Blue-Flowers, Granite Rock, Red Flats, Lightning-Split-Tree and South Mountain.

1. Give each student a length of rope or heavy twine. They may tie a knot on their "counting rope" each time they listen to or read the story.

2. The Indian names of places describe how the site looks or something that makes it special. Take a walk around your school grounds. Encourage the students to rename some of the places there.

3. Have the students take turns being blindfolded. Let them experience how their other senses help them sense what they cannot see. As they are led by their partner, inside or outside, they should use their ears and hands to investigate their surroundings.

Resources

Nonfiction

Jedrosz, Aleksander. *Eyes.* Mahwah, New Jersey: Troll Associates, 1992.

Parker, Steve. *The Eye and Seeing.* New York: Franklin Watts, 1989.

Ruis, Maria, J.M. Parramon, and J.J. Puig. *The Five Senses: Sight.* Hauppauge, New York: Barron's, 1985.

Sharman, Lydia. *The Amazing Book of Shapes.* London: Dorling Kindersley, 1994.

Showers, Paul. *Look at Your Eyes.* New York: HarperCollins Publishers, 1992.

Simon, Seymour. *The Optical Illusion Book.* New York: William Morrow and Company, 1984.

White, Laurence B., and Ray Broekel. *Optical Illusions.* New York: Franklin Watts, 1986.

Fiction

Aliki, *Feelings.* New York: Greenwillow Books, 1984.

Martin, Jr., Bill, and John Archambault. *Knots on a Counting Rope.* New York: Henry Holt and Company, 1987.

20   Sight

Braille Reading

Blind people read with their fingertips. Sets of raised dots make up the Braille alphabet.

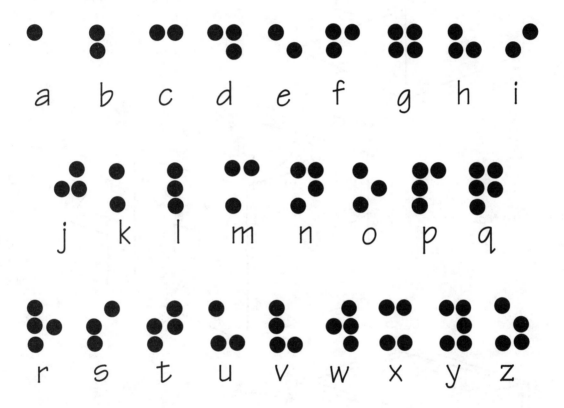

a b c d e f g h i

j k l m n o p q

r s t u v w x y z

To read the message below, place the activity page on a layer of newspapers. With a ballpoint pen, press firmly in each dot. When completed, turn the paper over and feel the Braille letters.

Pinhole Camera

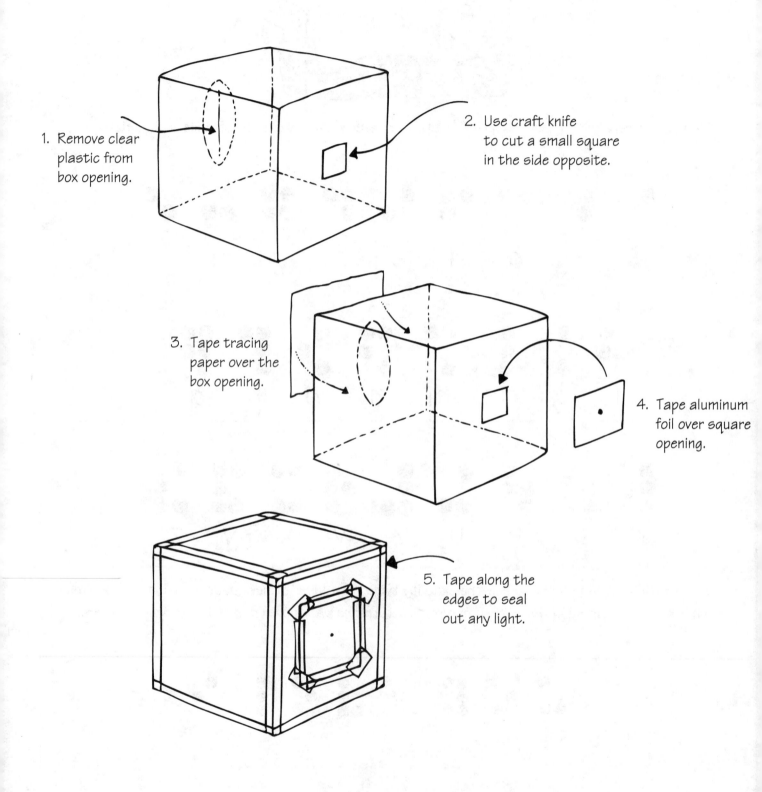

1. Remove clear plastic from box opening.

2. Use craft knife to cut a small square in the side opposite.

3. Tape tracing paper over the box opening.

4. Tape aluminum foil over square opening.

5. Tape along the edges to seal out any light.

Focus on Eyes

Be a cartoonist. See the suggestions below for drawing eyes and eyebrows. Experiment to create some cartoon characters of your own. See how many different expressions you can show on the heads below.

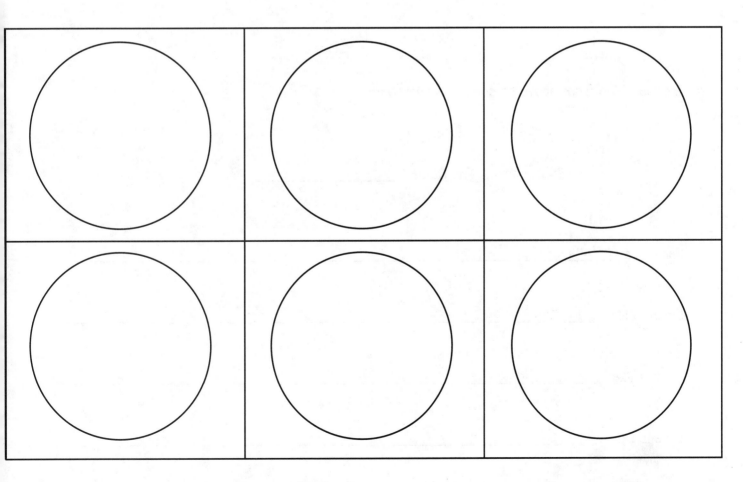

Name _____

Colors

Feels like

Sounds like

○ Color word ○

Tastes like

Smells like

Choose ideas from above to complete the poem.

The Color _____

Feels like _____.

Sounds like _____.

Tastes like _____.

Smells like _____.

Clip Art for Sight

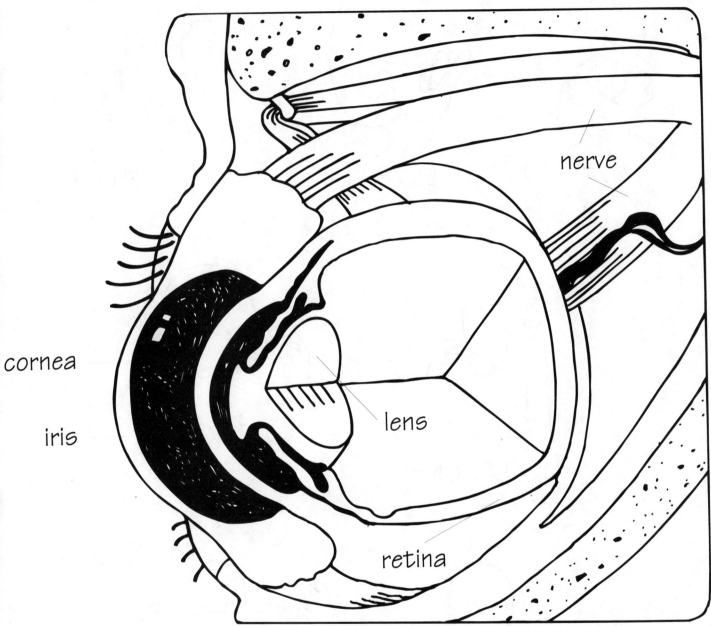

cornea

iris

lens

nerve

retina

Clip Art for Sight

LOVE

I LOVE YOU

HELLO

TELEPHONE

FUNNY

BOOK

WEIRD

Hearing

Nature Connection

Do You Know?

How do your ears work?

Why do loud sounds hurt your ears?

Why do dogs hear sounds you can't?

CLANG

CLANG

CLANG

Teacher Background

Whenever two objects are struck together they vibrate, sending sound waves through the air. Sound waves enter your ear through the ear canal. When they reach the eardrum, the waves set it in motion, which in turn vibrates the three tiny bones strung across the middle ear. The oval window, a membrane like the eardrum, leads into the inner ear. The cochlea, coiled like a snail, is about the size of a pea. It contains thousands of special hearing cells that transmit the vibrations to the brain by way of the auditory nerve. The brain identifies the sound you hear.

Information

Sounds are all around you. There are sounds you like to hear, like the voice of a friend. Some sounds are scary, especially at night when you don't know what's making them. Loud sounds can hurt your ears.

Your ears tell you a lot about your environment. You could walk in the woods and hear a rushing stream before you ever saw it. A bell ringing at a railroad crossing tells you to be careful, a train is coming down the tracks. If your cat is lost, you might hear it mewing in a tree.

Vibrations travel through the air without being seen, but you hear them with your ears. They are like rings that appear when you throw a rock in the water, but these rings are invisible. You can't see them with your eyes, but your ears hear them.

Your outer ear, the part you can see, collects sound waves and sends them into your ear canal, a tunnel that leads to your eardrum. When the sound waves reach the eardrum, they make it vibrate or move back and forth quickly. Loud sounds make it vibrate faster.

The middle ear, with three tiny bones, is on the other side of the eardrum. One is shaped like a hammer, one like an anvil and the other like a stirrup. When the eardrum vibrates, the little bones begin to jiggle and bump against the oval window leading to the inner ear. In the inner ear, a curled-up tube filled with liquid and lined with tiny hairs picks up the vibrations and sends the message to your brain. Your brain lets you know how to react. If it's a loud noise, you might cover your ears. If it's a soft sound, you might cup your ear to hear better.

People who are born deaf cannot hear. Others become deaf because of an illness or accident. Since they can't hear, they learn other ways to communicate. Sometimes they read lips. Maybe you have seen them using sign language.

Talk About

What sounds do you like to hear?

Can you name some warning sounds?

— Words to Know —

cochlea	inner ear	outer ear	vibrate
eardrum	middle ear	sound waves	vibrations

Literature Connection

Polar Bear, Polar Bear, What Do You Hear?, by Bill Martin, Jr.,
pictures by Eric Carle. New York: Henry Holt and Company, 1991.

Summary

A visit to the zoo introduces visitors to many sounds. It calls for imitations, repetitions and lots of fun.

Getting Ready

1. Name some animals you would like to see in the zoo.
2. What sounds would you hear?

Reading the Story

Imagine visiting a zoo. Listen to the animals as they roar and hiss and make their own distinctive sounds.

Thinking About the Story

Use the following questions to review the story and investigate the plot:

1. Name the animals in the story. What sounds does each make?
2. What would an elephant's trumpet sound like or the hiss of a boa constrictor?

Activities to Try

Choral Reading

Prepare a three-part choral reading of the story. One part of the group asks the question, one gives the answer and the third provides the sounds. Rotate so everyone has a turn doing each part.

What Do You Hear?

Talk about other animals you could see at the zoo. What noises do they make? Have the students complete the top half of page 42, using new animals and sounds to fill in the blanks.

Sentence Building

Look at the bottom half of page 42. Demonstrate how to answer questions in full sentences. Help them transfer their ideas from either exercise on page 42 to a booklet format.

Combining Words and Phrases

Write the following lists of words and phrases on sentence strips so they may be manipulated in a pocket chart. Use a different color pen to write each list of words.

Animals

seals	tigers	monkeys	parrots
snakes	gorillas	lions	alligators

Sounds

hiss	howl	growl	roar
grunt	bark	squawk	squeal

Places

in the tree.	on the beach.	near the water.
by the river.	from the hill.	in the jungle.
near the rocks.	behind the log.	from the swamp.

Direct the students to use one strip from each set to complete a sentence.

Sample: Snakes hiss in the jungle.

Stuffed Animals

Materials
large patterns of zoo animals
12" x 18" (30 x 46 cm) white and colored construction paper, one sheet of white for the template and two sheets of colored for each student
paper clips
tempera paint
brushes
scissors
newspaper
stapler

Directions

1. Trace an animal on the white paper to make a pattern.

2. Use paper clips to hold the white pattern and two colored sheets together while cutting out the animal.

3. Study the animal patterns. Notice the simple lines, bright colors and textures. Imitate the style when you paint your animal.

4. Begin stapling the sides together before you start stuffing it with crumpled newspaper. Continue to stuff and staple until the animal has the desired shape.

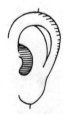

In the Barnyard

For a visit to the barnyard, distribute page 43 to the class. Have them follow directions to make flash cards to use at their desks.

1. Add more animals, sounds and places to the lists.

2. Write and illustrate your favorite sentences on a separate sheet of paper.

3. Select one sentence in the pocket chart to use as a story starter.

Expanded Sentences

Brainstorm to make a list of animals you might find at a circus, in the forest or at a pet store. Decide what kind of sound each makes. This will make a base sentence.

Sample: The dog growled.

Next think of a word to describe the animal and add an ending phrase to tell something more about the animal.

Sample: The small dog growled at the frightened rabbit.

Animals and Hearing

Why is it important for animals to have good hearing?

Animal ears come in all shapes and sizes. Many have no visible ears. Birds have no outer ears, but beneath their feathers are small openings behind their eyes. Rabbits have large ears that can be turned to pick up sounds coming from all directions. Many fish have a line running along the side of their body that picks up vibrations traveling through the water.

It is important for both hunter and the hunted to have good hearing. Animals, like lions and tigers, have to be able to hear as well as see the prey they are stalking. Animals who are hunted, like deer and mice, must be alert to the sounds of an approaching predator. A flap of a wing or a snapping branch may be the only warning of danger.

Discovery Experiences

☐ Vibrations and Sounds

Materials
container with a plastic lid
grains of rice
rubber band for each
student

Directions

Where do sounds come from?

1. Place the grains of rice on a lid. Lightly tap the lid with a pencil. What happened? Why did the rice dance? If you hit it harder, are the results the same?

2. Stretch a rubber band and pluck it. Observe what happens. Discuss what they see, feel and hear?

Explanation: Sounds are made when something vibrates. We hear sounds when our ears pick up vibrations moving through the air.

CLICK
CLACK

☐ Two Ears vs. One

Can you tell from what direction a sound is coming when you use only one ear?

Directions: Select a student to sit together with his or her eyes closed. When you tap two pencils together he or she should determine from which direction the sound is coming—front or back, right or left side, above or below, near or far.

Next, have the child cover one ear and repeat the procedure. How well can he or she determine the direction of the sound using only one ear?

Explanation: Sound waves don't reach both ears at the same time. With two ears we can better pinpoint the direction from which a sound originates and how far away it is.

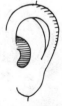

32 Hearing

Identify the Sound

Place mystery items, such as buttons, beans pennies, paper clips, beads and rice in covered containers. How well can the children guess the objects from shaking the containers?

Shake the container and have one child at a time guess what's inside. Supply a clue when necessary. Let them make up clues as well.

Match the Sound

Materials
several small, opaque containers with lids (the number will depend on the age and ability of the group)
small items such as beans, rice, gravel, paper clips, pins and nails

Directions

Prepare two containers of each item. Small groups of students may work together to match like items by shaking the containers and listening to the noise made by the contents.

Variation: Use the containers to play a game similar to Memory. Explain to the class that sounds are to be matched. Players take turns. If they successfully pick up a pair that matches, they may keep them. If not, the containers remain on the table and the next person tries. Whoever has the most pairs at the end of the game is the winner.

crackle

crunch

Crackle and Snap

Give each student a sheet of paper. How many sounds can they make with the piece of paper? They may change the shape and appearance of the paper as they discover different sounds. Discuss the activity. Record on a chart the ways they made noise with the paper.

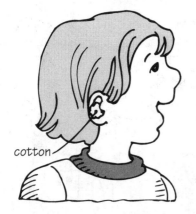

cotton

What Does It Sound Like?

Have the students put cotton in both ears. While they can still hear, it simulates the experience of the hearing impaired.

Direct them to continue their normal activities. Discuss what they learned from the activity. How did they feel?

What Did You Hear?

A blind person depends more on hearing than a sighted person. Have the students work in pairs. While one is blindfolded, the other leads him or her around a designated area. Can they tell where they are by listening to the sounds around them? Change places and discuss.

String Phones

Materials
2 paper cups
string
2 paper clips

Directions

Have each student work with a partner.

1. Thread each end of the string through a small hole in the bottom of the cup.

2. Tie the string around a paper clip to keep it from pulling out.

3. Stretch the string so it is pulled taut between the cups.

4. Take turns speaking into the cup in a soft voice and listening to a partner with the cup held over the ear.

Follow-Up

1. What happens if the string isn't pulled tightly?

2. How would you go about connecting two sets of phones to carry on a four-way conversation? (Answer: Cross the lines from the two sets. The second line should loop over the first and be pulled taut.)

34 Hearing

Suggested Activities

Different Kinds of Sound

Make lists of loud sounds, sounds you like to hear, sounds you don't like and scary sounds.

Divide the class into four groups. Each group should list one type of sound. Share the results of the brainstorming.

Incorporate some of the ideas into a story. Some titles are suggested.

The Buzzy Bee   *Talking Pets*

An Unusual Noise   *The Loudest Hoot*

Quiet/Noisy

Read *The Quiet Noisy Book*, by Margaret Wise Brown.

1. Have the students select their favorite quiet sound from the book.

2. Make a list of other quiet sounds.

3. Select one of the sounds to feature in a class book of quiet sounds. They may draw a picture, compose a poem or write a description of their sound.

4. Think of some quiet things that happen in nature, like flowers blooming or the sun setting. Draw a picture of things that don't make any noise as they change.

How Well Do You Listen?

No matter how well ears work, if a person isn't listening, he or she won't hear. Discuss reasons why people don't listen. Talk about the importance of listening.

A Listen Walk

Before the group begins their walk, have them predict what sounds they will probably hear. Stop along the way and notice the sounds. Close your eyes to concentrate on hearing things near and far.

At the end of the walk have the class work in small groups to list the sounds they heard. They may list their ideas under the headings:

People   Animals   Machines   Others

What Sounds Do You Hear?

Select one location featured in the handout on page 44 and discuss sounds you would expect to hear. List their ideas on a chart for further reference.

Divide the class into eight groups. Each group is responsible for brainstorming ideas for one location. Have them list their ideas on a large chart that can be shared with the entire class.

Discuss sounds that could be heard in the various locations pictured on the worksheet.

Choose one of the activities listed below to complete.

    a. Students may select three or four of the pictures to illustrate pages of a booklet. They may add captions, list sounds that could be heard there or tell something about each place.

    b. Have them fold a 4¹/₂" x 6" (11 x 15 cm) sheet of paper into thirds. Paste one of the scenes in the center panel. Show what happened before and after in the first and last sections. For example, if the picture of the park is used, what would it look like before people arrived and after they left?

Ears Hear

Read "Ears Hear," in *Read-Aloud Rhymes for the Very Young*. Every line mentions a person, place or thing and a sound associated with each. Help the students discover other combinations. They should not be concerned with trying to rhyme.

Trains

1. Read *Train Song*, by Diane Siebert, to the class. Listen to the clickety-clack along the tracks as trains rumble through cities and crisscross the countryside. Enjoy the rhymed text and painted illustrations.

2. Have the students relate personal experiences while traveling on trains or watching them pass.

Sound Poem

Create a poem. Share the following words with the students:

splash	buzz	hiss	whir	thump	swish
squeak	whoosh	crash	pop	creak	zing
zap	splat	kerplop	crackle	clang	pow

Have the students listen to the words and say them together. Encourage them to think about what things and actions make these noises, and experiment arranging them in different ways.

Catch the Wind

Create a mobile that catches the breezes and produces musical tones. Wind chimes should be pleasing to the ears and attractive to the eyes.

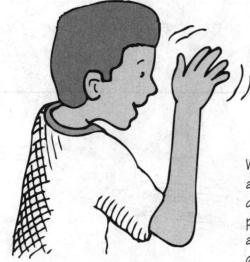

Communication

When you talk to each other, you communicate. You talk about what you did, who you saw, what you are planning to do and places you have visited. You listen to what other people say. You hear their questions and comments, hopes and wishes. When people communicate, they use words and gestures to let each other know what's going on.

Sign Language

Share the poem "Deaf Donald," from *A Light in the Attic*, by Shel Silverstein, with the class. Choral read with two groups reciting/signing alternating lines.

Hear/Here

Homophones are words that sound the same but have a different spelling and meaning. *Hear* and *here* are homophones, so are *to*, *too* and *two*. What other homophones can you think of?

1. Illustrate and label pairs of homophones for a bulletin board.
2. Write sentences using homophones.

Sample: Did you see the deep blue sea?

Music and Art

Materials
tape of instrumental music
finger paints
crayons
markers
paper

Directions

What does music look and feel like?

Encourage the children to paint and draw what they hear and feel while listening to the music. Have them talk about their pieces of artwork.

Music and Movement

Materials

tapes of different types of music

Directions

Have the students listen and move to the tempo of the music. Suggest they improvise and try different steps.

The Tube Band

Materials

toilet tissue tubes
waxed paper
rubber bands or tape
circle patterns (4" [10 cm] diameter)
rice or beans

Directions

1. To make a kazoo

    a. Use the pattern to cut a circle from a sheet of waxed paper.

    b. Secure the circle over one end with a rubber band or tape.

    c. Make a small hole ½" (1.25 cm) from the open end of the tube. Hum into the open end. You should be able to feel the vibrations when you lightly touch the waxed paper.

2. To make a finger drum

    a. Follow the directions for making the kazoo but omit the hole.

    b. Lightly tap with your fingers.

3. To make maracas

    a. Cut waxed paper circles for both ends of a tube.

    b. Cover one end of the tube and secure the waxed paper.

    c. Add 10 or 15 beans or several rice grains before covering the other end. Experiment using more beans or rice, or by mixing the two. Shake the maraca in time with the music.

Have the students "play" their instruments while listening to various rhythms.

Resources

Nonfiction

Barker, Wendy, and Andrew Haslam. *Sound.* New York: Aladdin Books, 1993.

Mathers, Douglas. *Ears.* Mahwah, New Jersey: Troll Associates, 1992.

Ruis, Maria, J.M. Parramont, and J.J. Puig. *The Five Senses: Hearing.* Hauppauge, New York: Barron's, 1985.

Showers, Paul. *Ears Are for Hearing.* New York: Thomas Y. Crowell, 1990.

Fiction

Brown, Margaret Wise. *The Noisy Book.* New York: HarperCollins Publishers, 1993.

Brown, Margaret Wise. *The Quiet Noisy Book.* New York: HarperCollins Publishers, 1993.

Martin, Bill. *Polar Bear, Polar Bear, What Do You Hear?* New York: Henry Holt and Company, 1991.

Prelutsky, Jack. *Read-Aloud Rhymes for the Very Young.* New York: Alfred A. Knopf Publishers, 1986.

Siebert, Diane. *Train Song.* New York: HarperCollins Publishers, 1990.

Silverstein, Shel. *A Light in the Attic.* New York: Harper & Row, 1981.

Name _____

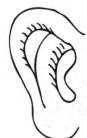 # What Do You Hear?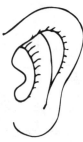

_____, _____, what do you here?

I hear a _____, _____, in my ear.

_____, _____, what do you hear?

I hear a _____, _____, in my ear.

Writing Questions and Answers

Select a zoo animal. Use the lines below to write questions and answers.

Sample: Why is the bear growling?

1. Why is the _____ _____ ing?

   The _____ is _____ing because

   _____.

2. Why is the _____ _____ ing?

   The _____ is _____ing because

   _____.

Name _____

In the Barnyard

Cut along the dotted lines to make flash cards. Use the flash cards to write sentences about farm animals.

Animals

Sheep	Cows	Chickens	Roosters	Horses
Pigs	Goats	Ducks	Chicks	Donkeys

Sounds

moo	crow	oink	quack	bray
baa	cluck	neigh	baa	peep

Places

in the field.	beside the barn.	in the pond.	from the tree.
by the tractor.	behind the coop.	under the hay.	in the mud.
on the fence.	in the garden.	in the meadow.	by the road.

On a separate paper, write and illustrate some of your sentences.

What Sounds Do You Hear?

on a playground

in the forest

in the country

in the rain

at the beach

in the park

at the circus

at night

at a ball game

Musical Instruments

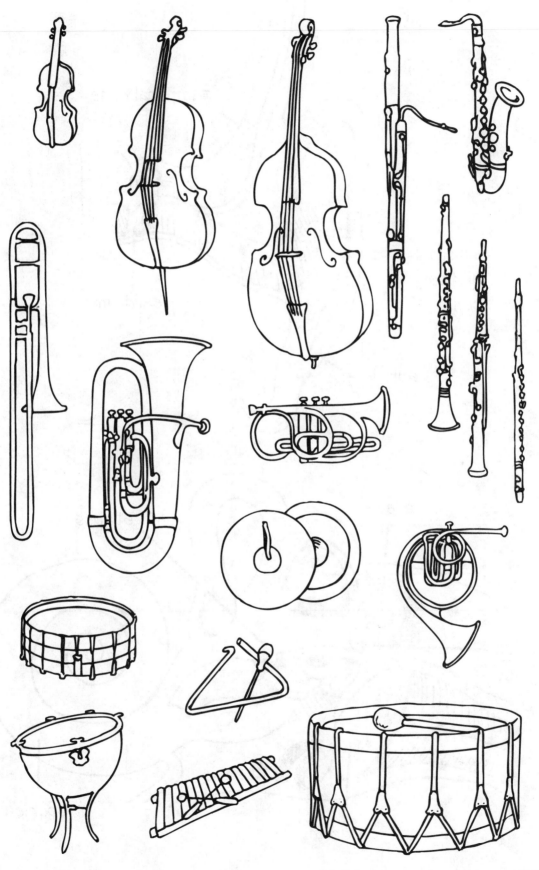

Clip Art for Hearing

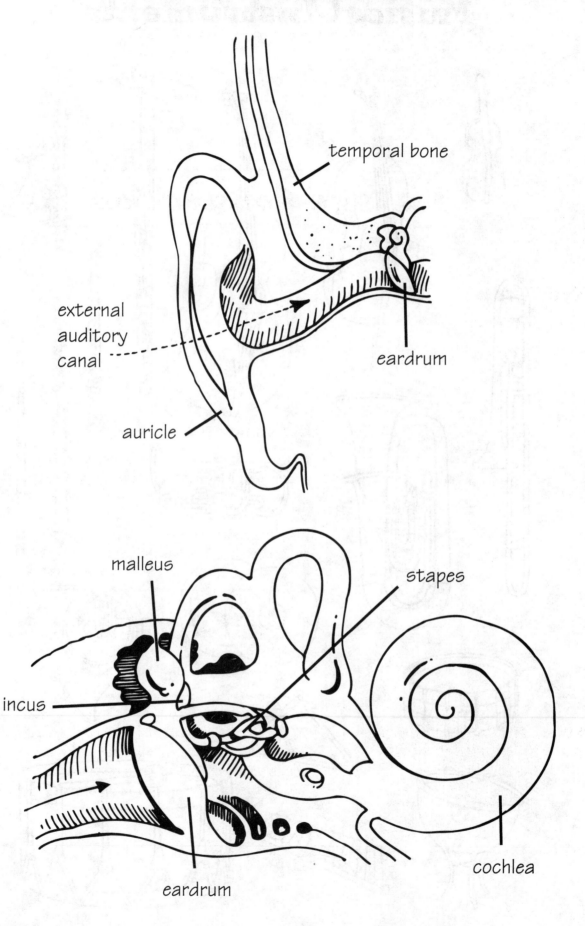

temporal bone

external
auditory
canal

eardrum

auricle

malleus

stapes

incus

eardrum

cochlea

Touch

Nature Connection

Do You Know?

How do you feel objects?

Are some areas more sensitive to touch than others?

Teacher Background

Sensory receptors are nerve endings that respond to touch, pain, pressure, heat and cold. They are located in or beneath the skin. Unlike other sense organs which are located in the head, sense receptors are scattered all over the body. Skin can detect touch, but some areas are more sensitive than others. There are more nerve endings for touch on our fingertips and lips. Sense receptors on our backs are spaced much farther apart.

When the receptors in our skin are activated, they send impulses along the cord to the brain. The brain sorts out the message and lets us know what we are feeling. Is it rough or smooth, hot or cold? Is there pain or danger?

The sense of touch is not as well understood by scientists as the other senses, but it is important. In some cases it could save us from more serious injury. After an encounter with barbed wire, our receptors send messages to the brain. The brain responds and lets us know how to react. In this case, to move slowly and carefully.

Information

When you see something, you may know from past experience that it is hard, rough, soft or silky. You learned that by using your sense of touch. The sense of touch may not seem as impressive as the others, but it does play an important role. In some cases your sense of touch could save you from serious injury. If you touch something hot, you quickly pull your hand away before you are seriously burned.

Some blind people use their sense of touch to read. They are able to tell the difference between letters and words by touching the raised bumps on a page.

Artists who make pottery feel the clay in their hands. They can tell if it is too damp or too dry. They know when the shape is right.

Did you ever wonder why babies always put things in their mouths? It is their way of discovering the world around them. Like fingers, lips are sensitive to touch. Babies will learn to use their other senses later.

Talk About

What can you learn about your surroundings by using your sense of touch?

What things do you like to feel?

Words to Know

pain   pressure   texture

48   Touch

Literature Connection

Seven Blind Mice, by Ed Young.

Summary   When seven blind mice found "a strange Something" by their pond, they were frightened. One by one, six of the mice went out to investigate. Each touched a different part and came back with a different theory. The seventh mouse made a more thorough investigation and concluded that when all the parts were put together, "the strange Something" was an elephant.

Getting Ready

1. If you were blind, how could you find out what was around you?

2. For a hands-on experience, have the children investigate an automobile or van while blindfolded. How well can they identify the parts they touch?

Reading the Story   Read *Seven Blind Mice* for enjoyment. Once a pattern is set, have the children hypothesize before revealing what each mouse thinks it is touching.

Thinking About the Story

Use the following questions to review the story and investigate the plot:

1. Why did all the mice run home when they first found a "Something" by their pond? What would you have done if you were in their place?

2. What did each mouse think he was touching? Can you name the six things?

3. Why were the mice not able to solve the mystery?

4. Why was the last mouse able to solve the mystery?

5. Was there another way they could have found out who was visiting?

Activities

1. Instruct the students to complete the activity on page 61. Use the same color crayon or marker to color the two items that match. For example, the tail and rope could be colored blue.

2. As a teacher-directed activity, draw a picture of the pond visitor as the mice imagined it. Instead of legs, it would have pillars. Spears would take the place of tusks, etc.

3. Prepare a flannel board story of *Seven Blind Mice*. Use the elephant and mouse patterns on pages 62 to 64. Retell the story with the help of the children. They may manipulate the felt pieces to create their own stories.

Seven Blind Mice

4. Discuss ideas for story extenders. What happened after the mice discovered it was an elephant who was visiting their pond? Did they try to make it go away? How could they do that? Could a mouse become friends with an elephant? Suppose the elephant let the mice climb up its legs, swing on its tail and slide down its tusks. Encourage the students to compose a story using some of the ideas generated in the discussion.

5. Reproduce a copy of the elephant pattern on page 64 for each student. They may color the elephant and add background details. Have them write or dictate an explanation of what is taking place in their illustration. Assemble a class book to publish or use separately as a bulletin board display.

6. Read aloud the poem, "The Blind Men and the Elephant." Compare it to the *Seven Blind Mice*. Discuss the similarities and differences of the two tales.

7. Help the students make mice finger puppets. See page 65 for a pattern. The puppets may be used to practice oral speaking skills and to engage in creative dramatics. Refer to the handout for additional ideas.

50 Touch

Discovery Experiences

Bring in items for a "Please Touch" exhibit. Students may have additional articles they would like to contribute to the display.

We usually depend on our eyes to help us identify objects. Using only the sense of touch, how well can familiar objects be identified? Try the following activities with the class to strengthen their tactile discrimination and develop their vocabularies.

☐ What Is It?

Materials
blindfold
variety of small objects to feel and identify

Directions

Place an item in the hand of a blindfolded student. He should describe how it feels, what he thinks it is used for and identify it. If necessary, other members of the class may take turns giving hints.

☐ What's in the Bag?

Materials
objects such as an apple, lemon, potato, button, tennis ball, cotton ball, seashell, rock
paper or opaque plastic bags, one for each group

Directions

Place one object at a time in the "mystery bag." Have the children take turns reaching into the bag. They should describe what they feel without telling what it is. Is it smooth, sharp, big or small? What shape is it? From the description, can other students guess what is in the bag?

☐ Hot or Cold?

Materials

3 bowls for each group

hot* and cold water (*just warm enough to identify as "hot" with a finger)

Directions

1. Pour hot water in one bowl, cold in another and mix hot and cold in the third.

2. Have each student place one finger in the hot water and one in the cold, and leave it there for at least a minute. When time is up, put both fingers in the warm water.

   a. How does the water feel on their skin?

   b. Do both fingers feel the same?

   c. Can they explain what has happened?

3. Do the experiment again but omit the warm water. How does it feel to go from hot to cold and cold to hot? Using what was learned in the experiments, discuss why water feels cold when you first get in a swimming pool?

☐ Sorting

Materials

buttons

geometric shapes of various sizes

leaves

seashells

blindfold

Directions

Have individual class members take turns sorting a group of objects while they are blindfolded, using only the sense of touch. They should decide how to separate items in the group. Will it be by texture, size or shape? Can someone else guess the categories?

52   Touch

Suggested Activities

Rubbings

Materials

textures that can be used to show patterns, such as sample pages from wallpaper books
different grades of sandpaper from fine to coarse
pieces of wood with interesting grains
fabric
crayons (without paper)
paper

Directions

To make a rubbing

1. Place a sheet of paper on a textured surface.
2. Rub back and forth across the paper with the side of a crayon. The pattern will mysteriously appear.
3. Experiment by varying the amount of pressure used to make the color darker.
4. Use more than one crayon to blend colors.

For variety, go on a texture hunt in the classroom and outdoors. Discuss the different types of textures and where they were found.

Fantasy Fish

Give each student copies of pages 66 and 67 to complete. Following are some additional ideas that may be used with the fish patterns.

1. Instead of gluing the colored fish onto one background, direct the students to place one fish on each page of a booklet. They may select one idea from below.

   a. Invent fantasy fish facts and add them to the book.

   b. Write an adventure story starring the fish. Use one of the following titles or make up one of your own:

   An Underwater Hideaway   The Missing Fin

   Where's Sammy?

2. Create a mobile. After coloring the fish, the students may glue them to construction paper and cut them out, leaving a thin margin of color around each. Suspend them by thread at different levels from a wire coat hanger.

3. Make a mural. Enlarge the fish on a copier or have the students draw their own. Remind them to think big. Color as directed. Paint a background scene and attach the fish.

Making Comparisons

1. Introduce the following descriptive words to the students: *hard, soft, wet, dry, smooth* and *rough*.

2. Collect items that display these attributes, such as stuffed animals, model cars and small toys.

3. Make a list of items that would fit under each heading.

4. Have the students look through magazines to find and cut out pictures of things they can touch. Instruct them to place like items together. Can other students determine the category?

5. Discuss and assign the handout on page 68.

Big Book of Things to Feel

Members of the class may compile a book of things to touch.

1. Have the children collect samples of textures from around the house.

2. Model the procedure on a chart using page 69 as a guide.

3. After everyone has the opportunity to touch the sample, work through the page together.

   a. List words that describe the texture.

      Sample: sandpaper—rough, bumpy, coarse

   b. Name some other things that are rough.

      Sample: shark's skin, cat's tongue, tree bark

   c. Refer to the list to compose descriptive sentences.

      Sample: The cat's tongue felt rough against my hand.

4. Demonstrate how these ideas can be transferred to a large sheet of paper. Instead of listing the words and sentences as they appear on the worksheet, they should be arranged creatively.

5. Give a copy of page 69 to each student. Each small group should list its ideas and decide how to design and complete a page for the big book.

BIG BOOK OF THINGS TO FEEL

54   Touch

Fingerprints

Everyone has fingerprints that are different from anyone else's. Have the children examine their fingertips under a magnifying glass. The ridges help them get a better grip on things with their hands. Fingerprints can also be used to identify people.

Fingerprints Plus

Materials
ink pad (washable ink)
paper
felt-tipped marking pens

Directions

Direct the students to experiment using their thumb and fingerprints to make prints on paper. They may add a few lines to create people, insects and animals.

Refer to *Ed Emberley's Great Thumbprint Drawing Book* for ideas.

Sandpaper Transfers

Materials

Materials
crayons
sandpaper
paper
iron (Adult use only!)

Directions

Have the students color directly on the sandpaper. Place a sheet of smooth paper on the sandpaper. Press with a warm iron. Display both the transfer and the original.

Note: The heat of the iron will change the texture of the crayon.

Clay

Directions

Let the students feel the clay respond to their fingers as they create with their hands.

Have the students knead the clay to make it more pliable and remove air bubbles. They may then explore one of the following methods:

1. Start with a ball and mold it to form an animal. (Pieces that are stuck on afterwards tend to crack while drying.)

2. Roll out a ball of clay to make a ½" (1.25 cm) thick slab. Use cookie cutters to cut out shapes. Designs may be etched with a sharp tool.

Allow the pieces to air dry for a few days, then paint with tempera paint and coat with clear acrylic.

Materials

Materials
water-based clay
rolling pin
cookie cutters
plastic knives
tools for etching designs

56   Touch

Literature Connection

King Midas and the Golden Touch, by Nathaniel Hawthorne, as retold by Kathryn Hewitt.

Introduction

When we touch something, we can feel if it is soft, hard, hot, warm or cold. In the story, King Midas' touch turns something cold and hard.

Read the myth aloud and examine the illustrations for details. Discuss the questions to recall the story and encourage critical thinking. The activities may be worked on individually or in groups.

Summary

King Midas loved gold more than almost anything else in the world. When he was given a wish, he asked that everything he touched be turned to gold. It seemed like a good idea at the time. When his beloved daughter, Marigold, was turned into a golden statue, he came to his senses. Fortunately, the stranger who first granted him his wish returned and told him how to undo the spell. Midas would be the first to tell you to be careful what you wish for, because your wish may be granted.

Do You Remember?

1. In the beginning of the story, what did King Midas do during the day?

2. Why was Midas disappointed when he first tried to use his Golden Touch?

3. Name some things that King Midas turned into gold.

4. What made Midas realize that gold wasn't as important to him as he first thought?

Thinking About the Story

1. What things became completely useless after they were touched by Midas?

2. What if the mysterious stranger had not returned to rid Midas of his Golden Touch?

3. What lesson did the King learn?

Activities to Try

1. Describe King Midas at the beginning of the story and at the end.

2. Illustrate three or four scenes from the story. Write a short explanation of each drawing. Bind the pictures and description to make a book.

3. Pretend you are King Midas. Select one of the following scenes to dramatize:
   a. You are in your underground room admiring your golden treasures.
   b. You are surprised by a mysterious stranger who grants you one wish.
   c. You discover you can turn everything into gold.
   d. You just turned Marigold into a golden statue.
   e. You are returning from the river with a pitcher of water.
   f. You tell your grandchildren about a foolish man you once knew who had a Golden Touch.

4. Read "What Is Gold?" in *Hailstones and Halibut Bones*, by Mary O'Neill.
   a. Name some golden objects mentioned in the poem.
   b. List things that are colored gold that were not mentioned.
   c. Write a "Gold Is . . . " poem. Refer to the list for ideas.
   d. Mix yellow and orange together to paint a golden picture.

5. Create a golden collage. Search through magazines for pictures that show gold items. Be sure to include things that come from nature or are man-made.

6. Play King Midas Tag. It is similar to Freeze Tag, but when tagged, a person turns into a golden statue. Decide on the rules, but don't make too many.

Now Try This

1. Tell a story to explain what happened after you did one of the things mentioned above.

2. Select one of the animals in the poem on page 59. Read to discover more information about it. Report what you found most interesting.

3. Design a poster to remind people of the danger of not respecting wild animals.

58   Touch

Do Not Touch the Animals

Read the following poem to the class. Have them choose an activity to complete.

Never pet a porcupine.
Never poke a skunk.
Never grab a tiger's tooth,
Or squeeze an elephant's trunk.

Porcupines have prickly spines.
A skunk's scent smarts and stings.
Tigers' teeth are razor sharp.
Elephants remember things.

Never punch a crocodile.
Never pinch a rat.
Never whack a sleeping bear,
Or tickle a bob-tailed cat.

Crocodiles have mighty tails.
Rats have strong, sharp claws.
Bears don't like to wake up fast.
Bob-tailed cats have wicked jaws.

Resources

Nonfiction

Emberley, Ed. *Ed Emberley's Great Thumbprint Drawing Book*, New York: Scholastic Books, 1977.

Otto, Carolyn. *I Can Tell by Touching*. New York: HarperCollins Publishers, 1994.

Pluckrose, Henry. *Thinking About Touching*. London: Franklin Watts, 1986.

Ruis, Maria, J.M. Parramon, and J.J. Puig. *The Five Senses: Touch*. Hauppauge, New York: Barron's, 1989.

Fiction

Hewitt, Kathryn. *King Midas and the Golden Touch*. San Diego: Harcourt Brace Jovanovich Publishers, 1987.

O'Neill, Mary. *Hailstones and Halibut Bones*. New York: Doubleday, 1989.

Young, Ed. *Seven Blind Mice*. New York: Philomel Books, 1992.

Name _____

Seven Blind Mice Matching

Use the same color crayon or marker to match each pair of pictures.

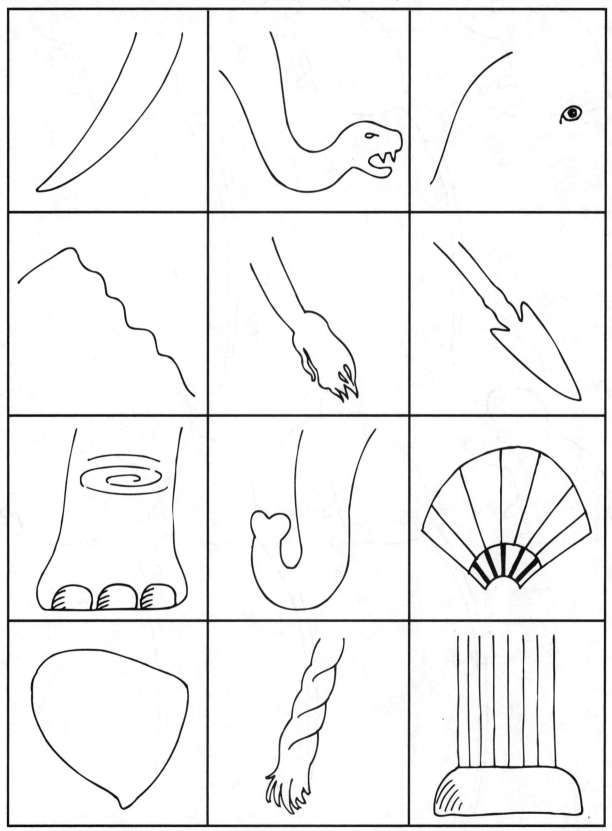

Touch **61**

Flannel Board Patterns

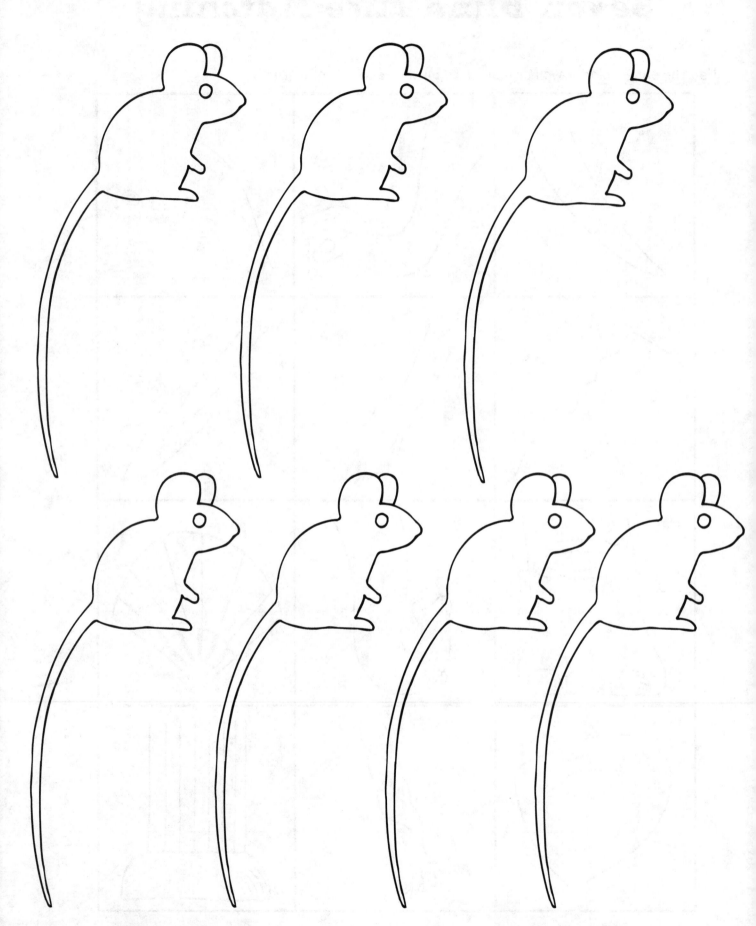

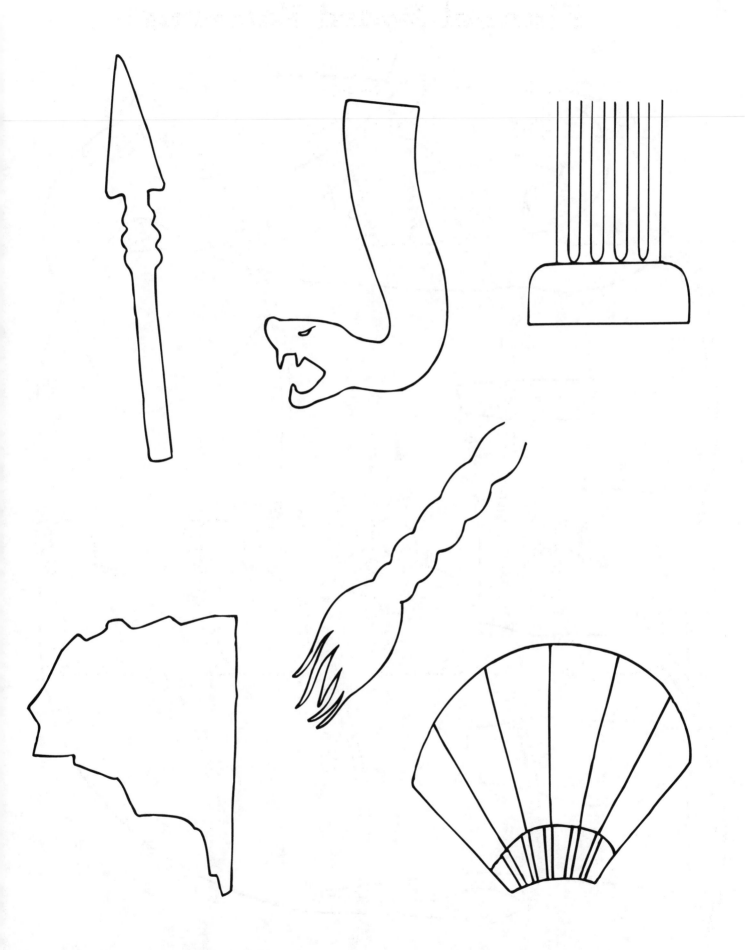

Touch   **63**

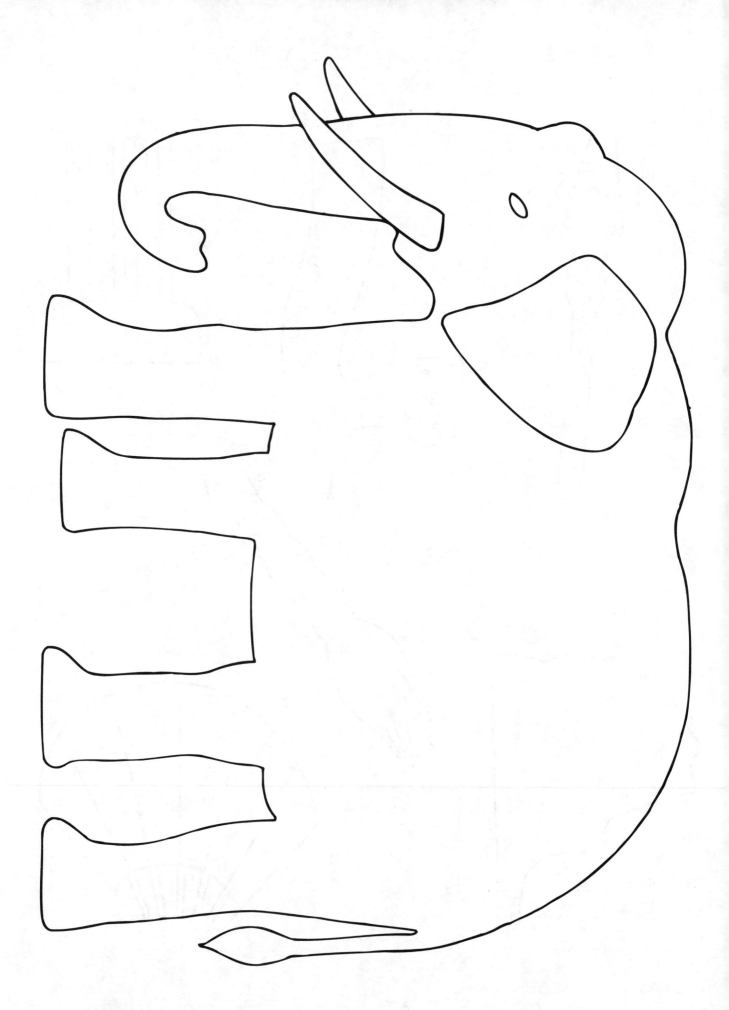

64   Touch

Mice Finger Puppets

Materials: *colored construction paper, scissors, glue or tape, yarn, stapler*

Directions: Help the children trace and cut out the mouse patterns. Adjust the puppet to the child's finger and tape or glue the cylinder closed. Attach a piece of yarn for the tail.

Note: For a more permanent puppet, use felt instead of construction paper and sew instead of glue.

Story Connection: Tell what your mouse thought it discovered when it went to investigate and what it really turned out to be.

Whole Language Connection: Write and perform a class story about the adventures of the "Rainbow Mice."

Fantasy Fish

Materials: crayons, various textures, scissors, light blue construction paper, glue

Directions: 1. Color each fish by placing the paper on a textured surface and rubbing a crayon across it to pick up the pattern. It is not necessary to stay inside the lines.

2. Cut the fish out and arrange on construction paper. Glue in place. Add details to complete an underwater scene.

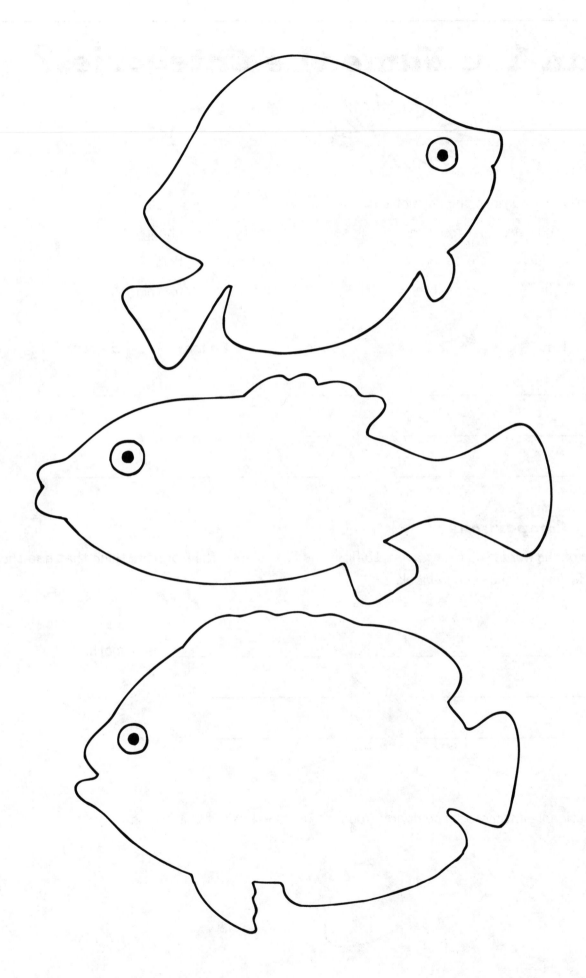

Touch **67**

Name _____

Can You Name the Categories?

Put the following words in the correct categories:

coarse	freezing	glossy	frosty	shaggy
sleek	satiny	jagged	sizzling	fiery
fluffy	molten	flat	icy	feathery

Hot	**Cold**	**Soft**	**Rough**	**Smooth**
_____	_____	_____	_____	_____
_____	_____	_____	_____	_____
_____	_____	_____	_____	_____

Making Comparisons

Use some of the words you wrote above to fill in the first blank. Think of something that has the opposite feeling for the second blank.

Sandpaper is _____, but a _____ is smooth.

A cat is _____, but a _____ is rough.

Snow is _____, but _____ is hot.

Write additional sentences to compare. You may use the back of this paper.

Name _____

 # How Does It Feel?

Glue sample here.

Words to describe how it feels

_____   _____   _____   _____

_____   _____   _____   _____

_____   _____   _____   _____

Other things that are _____

_____   _____   _____

_____   _____   _____

Sentences

_____

_____

_____

Clip Art for Touch

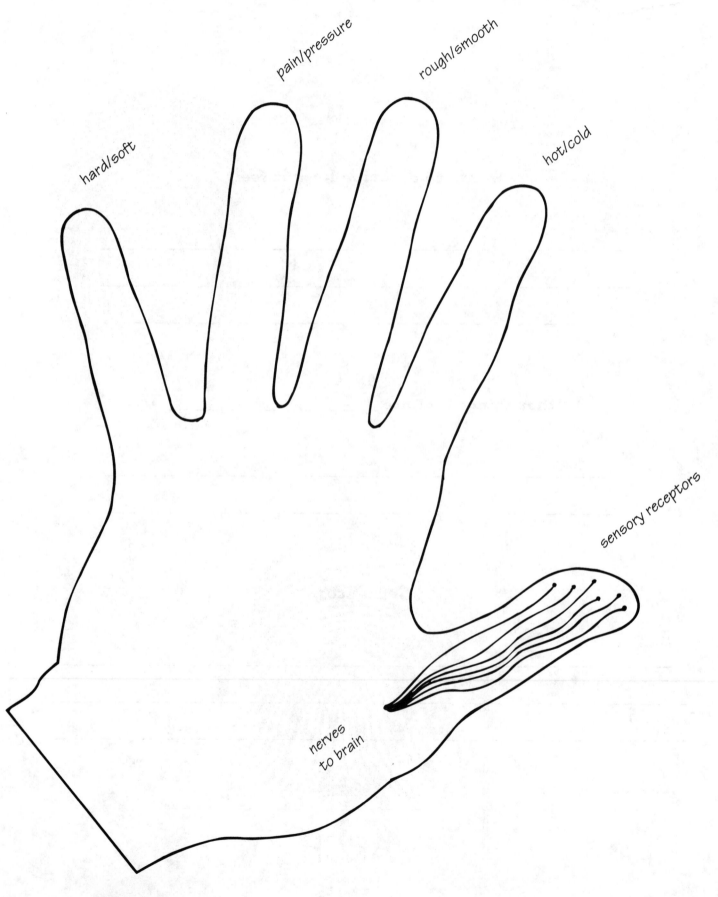

hard/soft

pain/pressure

rough/smooth

hot/cold

sensory receptors

nerves
to brain

Clip Art for Touch

LOOP

WHORL

ARCH

Taste

Nature Connection

Do **You Know?**

Where are your taste buds?

Why are children less eager to try new foods?

Teacher **Background**

Thousands of taste buds cover the tongue, making it look like the surface of a naval orange. Other taste buds are scattered on the roof of the mouth and at the back of the throat. The tongue's job is to detect flavors.

When the chemicals found naturally in foods are dissolved by saliva in the mouth, the taste buds respond. Small pores allow the saliva to reach the receptor cells within the taste buds. There, nerve impulses are sent to the brain, which identifies the taste.

Different parts of the tongue are sensitive to different tastes. Taste buds toward the tip of the tongue detect sweet tastes. Bitter flavors are registered at the back. Salty and sour taste receptors are located on the sides of the tongue, the former toward the front and the latter toward the back.

Children have more taste buds than adults, which is why they are probably more sensitive to hot and spicy flavors. Some tastes are also acquired. Adults are more adventurous when it comes to trying new tastes.

Before engaging in any of the tasting activities, please be aware of any food allergies your students may have.

Information

You taste things with your tongue. The tongue is covered with tiny bumps which are called taste buds. Different areas of the tongue respond to bitter, salty, sour and sweet tastes.

Long ago, when your ancestors were investigating the world around them, their sense of taste was very important. They learned to avoid new foods if they didn't taste right, especially if they were bitter. How food smelled was important, too. Today we are familiar with most available foods.

Your parents aren't really being mean to you when they serve you green things that grow in the vegetable garden. Some tastes have to be acquired. You may not like to eat some things at first. Eventually you may learn to like them, but if you don't try them, you'll never know.

Lots of times you are able to taste more than one flavor at a time. When you eat a cheeseburger, you experience different tastes. You enjoy the sweetness of the catsup and the sourness of the pickle. How would you describe the meat and cheese? You might use one word to describe the meal, *delicious*.

When you have a stuffy nose, you might think something is wrong with your taste buds, because you can't taste very well. Your taste buds are working fine. They send the usual messages to the brain. It's your sense of smell that is letting you down. The two senses work so closely that when you can't smell food, it seems as if you can't taste it either.

Eat your vegetables. They're good for you . . .

Talk About

What would it be like if you couldn't taste anything?

Name some foods that are sweet, sour, bitter or salty.

Words to Know

bitter	flavor	salty	sour	sweet	taste buds

Literature Connection

Everybody Cooks Rice, by Norah Dooley.

Summary

When a girl goes in search of her younger brother at dinnertime, she visits her neighbors' homes. She finds while each is having rice, their meals are quite different. The neighbors have come from many countries and have different backgrounds. They use traditional methods and special herbs and spices to prepare the rice dishes of their homelands.

Teacher Background

Rice is a grass. Other members of the grain family include wheat, oats, barley and corn. To grow rice, a warm climate is needed, along with an abundant amount of fresh water, either from rainfall or irrigation.

The growing fields, or paddies, are surrounded by levees that can be regulated to keep the water in or out. During the growing season the paddies are flooded. At harvesttime they are drained.

Rice seeds are planted in nursery beds that are surrounded by water, where they sprout and begin to grow. In about a month they develop into seedlings, or small plants, that are ready to be transferred into the flooded paddies.

In three months the plants are fully grown. Small green flowers appear and are pollinated by the wind. When the plants turn from bright green to pale yellow, they are ready to harvest. The paddies are drained and the soil dries. On small farms in China and India, the rice plants are gathered by hand. On large farms, such as in the United States, machinery is used to harvest and thresh the rice. After the grain dries it is sent to the mill where it is prepared for market.

Getting Ready

1. Are there different kinds of rice?
2. How is rice cooked at your house? What other ingredients are included?

Reading the Story

Read the story together to learn about a few of the many rice dishes from around the world.

Thinking About the Story

1. What countries were mentioned? Can you find them on a map?
2. Have you eaten rice prepared like any featured in the story?

Activities to Try

International Food Festival

If possible, plan an International Food Festival featuring rice dishes. Invite parents and members of the community to prepare the recipes included in the book, as well as their own special rice dishes.

Materials
page 85
colored construction paper
(12" x 4½" [30 x 10 cm]),
one sheet for each
student
crayons or markers
scissors
glue

Directions

Accordion Book

1. Read and talk about the text and illustrations on page 85.
2. After the pictures are colored, cut the page apart along the lines.
3. Fold the construction paper into four equal parts. Turn one end back to make the accordion fold.
4. Glue each section onto one part of the accordion to make a booklet.

Note: Give more capable students larger sheets of paper (6" x 18" [15 x 45 cm]). They may use the pictures and write their own more detailed explanation of the development of the rice plant from seed to grain.

Materials
rice
tagboard
felt or fabric
pencil
glue
assorted trims and buttons

Rice Bags

Directions

Instead of beans, use rice to fill bags. They may be used to play games, or decorate and display.

Have the students place the pattern of their choice on a piece of felt and trace around it twice. After cutting out both shapes, apply glue to the edges leaving a 2" (5 cm) opening to add the rice. Press the two sides together and let dry. The bags should be half filled with rice and the remaining space glued shut.

Note: If the rice bags are to be used for games, the edges should be tightly stitched.

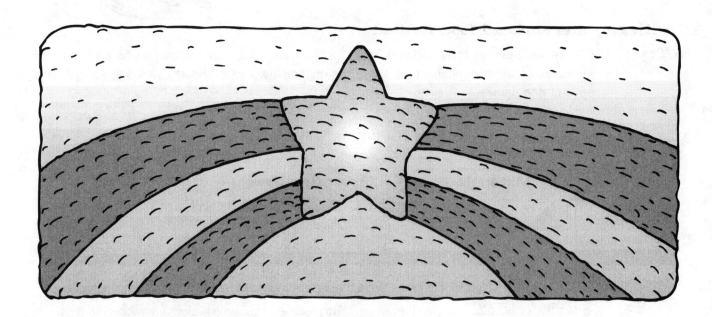

Materials
colored rice (see Note below)
cardboard
pencil
glue

Rice Mosaic

Directions

Have the students draw a simple design, abstract or representational on light cardboard. Direct them to apply a coat of glue to one area at a time and sprinkle colored rice over the prepared section. Repeat with different colors until the figure is covered with grains of rice. Allow the mosaic to dry overnight; then shake gently to remove excess rice.

Note: To color the rice, combine 1 tsp. (5 ml) food coloring and 1 cup (240 ml) cold water. Add the mixture to 2 cups (480 ml) uncooked rice. Let stand for five minutes then drain. Spread the rice on a cookie sheet and dry in a 250°F (120°C) oven for 15 minutes. Stir occasionally. Use more food coloring for a deeper color and less for a softer shade.

76 Taste

Discovery Experiences

☐ Taster's Choice

Raisin bran is manufactured by several companies. Select three brands to test. Set up a tasting center where a few children at a time may participate. For each person, you will need three paper cups, a spoon and three samples of cereal and milk. Label the cups A, B and C.

Hand out page 86 to record the results of the test. The leader may note the responses of younger children.

1. Have the children examine the contents of each cup. They should note the size, color and texture of the flakes and the number and size of the raisins.

2. When the milk has been added, have them rate the crispness of the flakes and the overall taste of the cereal.

3. After the test, have the children check the information on the box. How do they compare nutritionally? Are the ingredients the same? The order in which they are listed is important. The main ingredients are mentioned first.

4. Discuss the price of each brand. Was the most expensive brand also the favorite? Which was the best buy?

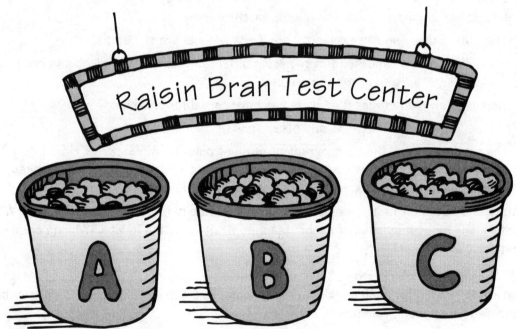

☐ Thumbs Up!

Besides cereal, crackers, chips and apples, a number of other items may be featured in taste tests. Prepare the food to be tasted and have the children decide which they prefer. Follow up with a discussion of the taste experience. What did they like and dislike about the flavors and textures?

Note: Additional Discovery Experiences, related to taste, may be found in the section featuring the sense of smell.

Suggested Activities

Have the students bring a variety of empty cereal boxes to school. Use them to discuss their favorite breakfast food, to compare and discuss nutrition facts and ingredients and to create a handy booklet.

And the Winner Is . . .

1. Conduct a survey to determine the most popular cereal and why it is preferred. Ask the class to respond to the following questions:

   a. What is your favorite cereal?

   b. Why do you like it? (tastes good, doesn't get soggy, good for me or other)

2. Make two bar graphs to show the results of the survey.

   Extra: a. Survey another class to see if the results are the same.

   b. Conduct another survey asking different questions. Collect and organize the information and graph the results.

   Sample: How many times a week do you have cereal for breakfast?

   Do you eat cereal at any other time of day?

3. Do the students think the main ingredient of most cereal is wheat, oats, rice or corn? Have them make a prediction before listing the cereals on a chart under the appropriate heading. Refer to the list of ingredients on each box. Note the first item mentioned.

4. Study the nutrition facts. Compare information about fat, sodium and sugar. Which cereals contain the most and least of each? Discuss healthy eating habits. Which cereal would be the best for them to eat?

5. Use the box to make booklet covers.

   Materials needed for each booklet: empty cereal box, two metal or plastic rings or colored yarn, lined or unlined paper, hole punch, scissors

   Directions:

   a. Remove the front and back panels from the box. These will become the covers of the booklet.

   b. Cut paper to fit the covers.

   c. Punch two holes in the covers and pages.

   d. Connect the pages with the rings or tie loosely with yarn.

78 Taste

A Serial

Unlike *cereal*, the breakfast food, a *serial* is a story told in more than one episode. At the end of each part the reader is left wondering what will happen next.

Have the children work in small groups to write a three-part story. The first two parts should end leaving the readers in suspense. The final installment should bring the tale to a definite conclusion.

New Tastes

Discuss with the class the pros and cons of trying new foods. Have them describe some pleasant experiences. Ask them how they feel about having to eat foods they don't like—even if they are good for them.

Read *The Boy Who Ate Around* aloud to the class. In this imaginative tale, Mo avoided eating string beans and cheese souffle by turning himself into a series of monsters that ate everything except what was on his plate.

Invent a Flavor

Collect and share lists of flavors from an ice cream parlor or grocery store freezer. Decide which names best describe the frozen treats. After explaining how flavors and textures combine to make a pleasing taste, brainstorm to make a list of possible combinations. Have the students individually or in small groups invent a new flavor combination and give it a name.

Flavor of the Day!

Survey the class to determine the favorite new flavor. Make a graph to show the results of the study.

Favorites

Have the students search magazines for pictures of food they enjoy. They may complete one of the assignments below:

1. Create a collage showing favorite foods.
2. Organize a booklet featuring favorites such as main courses, snacks and desserts.

To Whom It May Concern

After students select a favorite food product, have them write letters to the manufacturers. They should tell them why they like the product, how they think they could improve it or suggest a new flavor they think would be popular.

Fruit Salad

Assemble an assortment of fresh fruit such as apples, bananas, grapefruit, melon and grapes. Add canned or fresh pineapple chunks. The students, using plastic knives, can cut the fruit into bite-sized pieces and mix them together in a large bowl. Serve with a yogurt dressing. Eat and enjoy a medley of flavors and textures.

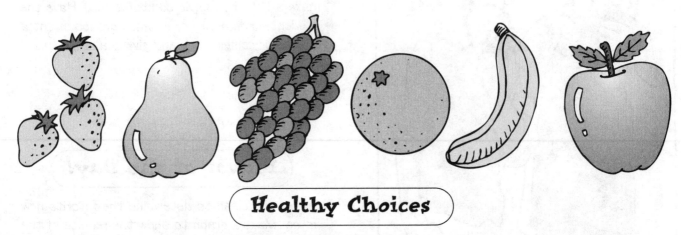

Healthy Choices

1. Discuss the Food Guide Pyramid, a guide to good eating habits. Are they eating the right kinds of food to stay healthy and grow strong?
2. Compile a class list of healthy treats that are nutritious and tasty.
3. Have the students keep a one-day record of the food they eat. Remind them to include snacks.

80 Taste

Tongue Twisters

The tongue detects flavors. It also helps us speak clearly. Our tongues sometimes get twisted when we tackle alliteration, words in a phrase or sentence that begin with the same sound.

1. See how quickly the students can repeat the sample sentences. How many times can they do it?

   Seven seals swam swiftly.

   Two tigers tasted tuna.

2. Help the children create additional tongue twisters.

How Is Your Memory?

Have the children imagine they are going on a picnic. Let them take turns adding to the basket. "We're going on a picnic and I'm bringing . . ." Each person, in turn, mentions what has previously been named then adds their contribution.

Watermelon: A Mini Unit

Watermelon is a summer treat best enjoyed outdoors on hot, sunny days. The watermelon can also be featured in a mini unit that explores creative writing activities.

Copy and distribute the watermelon poem on page 87.

Serve ice cold slices of watermelon to the students. Let them experience firsthand the sweet, sticky wonders of the fruit. Help them transfer their reactions into words to create prose and poetry.

Rhymes with Eat

Stomp your feet
To the beat
As you eat
In the heat
Oh so sweet
Watermelon!

Use the following list of words to create a poem. Each line of three syllables should end with one of the words listed below.

1. The pattern may be used to write about any food treat.

2. Write some couplets, two lines that rhyme and have the same beat.

Sample: When you're walking down the street,

You may see a friend to _____.

feet	beat	heat	meat	neat	beet
sleet	street	greet	meet	repeat	tweet
seat	cheat	athlete	complete	receipt	compete
wheat	sweet	defeat	treat	sheet	concrete

Green, Black and Red

What's red, black and green all over? Besides a watermelon, what else can you name? Compare the watermelon—fruit, rind and seeds—to other things that are red, green and black. Have small groups collaborate to make unusual comparisons. Encourage them to create similes that stretch the imagination.

Fruit as red as _____.

Rind as green as _____.

Seeds as black as _____.

82 Taste

Concrete Poem

A concrete poem is a kind of word picture. Instead of using lines to draw a picture, words are used.

To write a concrete poem about a watermelon, first draw a simple outline of the melon. Next, think of words and phrases that describe the watermelon or tell about its flavor. Arrange these words within or along the outline.

Have the students complete a concrete poem featuring the watermelon. Show them how to outline or fill in the shape with words.

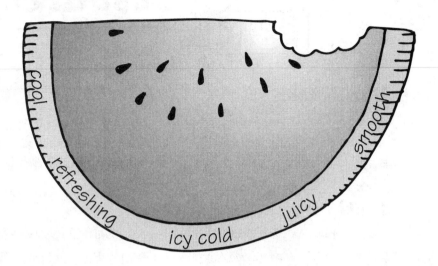

cool
refreshing
icy cold
juicy
smooth

What to Do with the Seeds

1. Count them. How many seeds are in one slice? In a whole watermelon?

2. Weigh them. How many seeds will it take to make an ounce? A gram?

3. Spit them. How far can you make them travel? How many feet? Yards? Meters? Measure the best of 10 tries.

4. Grow them. How long will it take them to begin to grow? Place a few seeds in a plastic bag with a damp paper towel and hang it by a window. Keep a record of their growth.

5. Wear them. After the seeds are washed and dried, string them on a thread to make a necklace.

Resources

Nonfiction

Haines, Gail Kay. *Sugar Is Sweet.* New York: Atheneum, 1992.

Johnson, Sylvia A. *Rice.* Minneapolis: Lerner Publishing Company, 1985.

Ruis, Maria, J.M. Parramon, and J.J. Puig. *The Five Senses: Taste.* Hauppauge, New York: Barron's, 1985.

Fiction

Dooley, Norah. *Everybody Cooks Rice.* Minneapolis: Carolrhoda Books, 1991.

Drescher, Henrik. *The Boy Who Ate Around.* New York: Hyperion Books, 1994.

Name _____

Rice from Seed to Grain

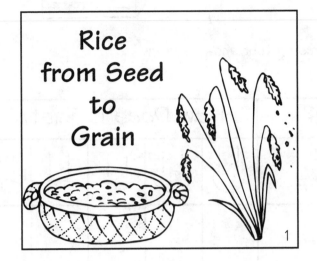

Rice
from Seed
to
Grain

1

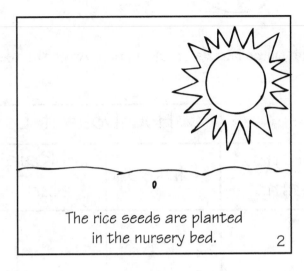

The rice seeds are planted
in the nursery bed.   2

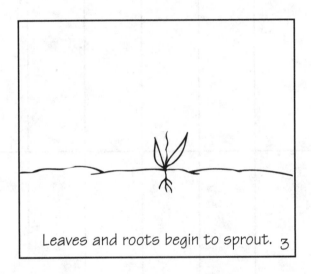

Leaves and roots begin to sprout. 3

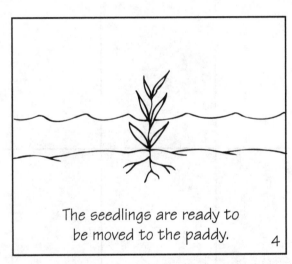

The seedlings are ready to
be moved to the paddy.   4

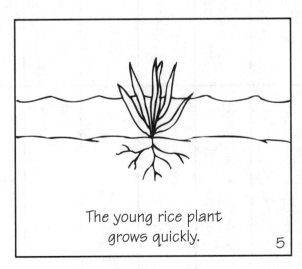

The young rice plant
grows quickly.   5

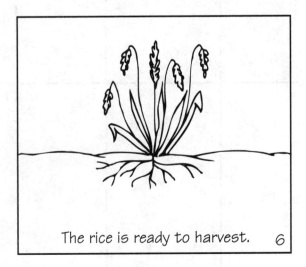

The rice is ready to harvest. 6

Taste **85**

Name _____

Taster's Choice

Test three brands of raisin bran. After the test, record your answers below.

Brand Name	How Does It Look?			How Does It Taste?				
	Flakes	Raisins size	#					
A								
B								
C								

Watermelon

Watermelon's good to eat
When you're searching for a treat
When you're standing on your feet
When you're sitting on your seat
When you're sweating from the heat.

Watermelon can't be beat
If you're trying to compete
If you're beating a retreat
If you're running in a meet
If you're dancing on concrete.

Watermelon, what a treat!
It's a fruit that's good to eat.
It's a special summer sweet.
It's a cool and tasty treat.
It's a way to beat the heat.

Patricia O'Brien

Clip Art for Taste

bitter

sweet

salty/sour

tongue

Clip Art for Taste

Smell

Nature Connection

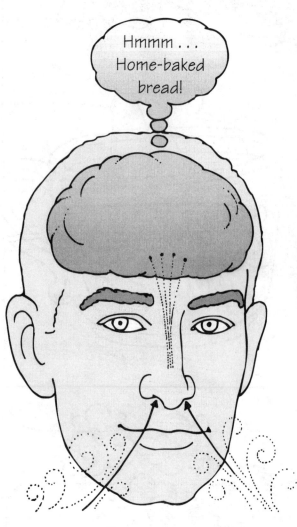

Hmmm . . . Home-baked bread!

Do You Know?

How does you nose work?

Why do your eyes water when you smell a freshly cut onion?

Teacher Background

Of the five senses, the sense of smell is the least complicated. Molecules floating through the air are inhaled through the nasal passage, where they stimulate the olfactory nerves in the upper part of the nostril. The information is transmitted to the brain. The brain translates the message, and the aroma is identified. Humans can identify thousands of different smells.

Before engaging in any of the smelling or tasting activities, please be aware of any allergies or sensitivities your students may have.

Information

Smells are all around you. They give you another way of sensing your environment. Odors travel through the air, but they are so small they can't be seen with your eyes. When you inhale, they travel into your nose. Nerves in your nose pick up the smell and send a message to your brain. Your brain lets you know how to react. If you're in a bakery, you may sniff the air, smile and say, "Mmmmmmmmmmm!" If you're outdoors and smell a skunk, you may hold your nose and say, "Yuck!"

Your sense of smell is useful. The smell of smoke could warn you of a fire. The smell of sour milk could stop you from drinking it. Your sense of smell gets tired and after a while you don't notice everyday smells.

Smells can remind you of places you have been and things you have done. Smoke from a fire might remind you of a time you roasted hot dogs in your backyard. It might also remind you of a house or forest fire.

Your senses of taste and smell are connected. When you have a stuffy nose, you can't smell or taste food very well. Pizza will feel hot or cold in your mouth, carrots will feel crunchy and mashed potatoes will feel smooth or lumpy. Maybe the best time to eat foods that are good for you, but you don't like, is when you have a cold.

Talk About

Do some people like smells that you don't like?

What smells remind you of things that happened in the past?

Words to Know

aroma   fragrance   nostril   odor   scent   spicy

Literature Connection

Mucky Moose, by Jonathan Allen.

Summary   Mucky Moose loved to wallow in the smelliest part of the swamp. His only friends, the birds, frogs and skunks, thought he smelled just fine. A wolf attempted to eat Mucky, but he couldn't stand the smell. He finally gave up when his plan to use a clothespin and gas mask didn't work. Mucky may not have smelled very good, but it kept him from being eaten.

Getting Ready
1. What is the worst thing you ever smelled?
2. Were you ever determined to do something but finally had to give up?
3. What made you change your mind?

Enjoy the Story   Read Mucky the Moose together. Enjoy the dialogue between the wolf and the moose.

Getting Ready
1. The following questions may be used to recall the story:
   a. Why was Mucky such a smelly moose?
   b. Who were his friends? What did they like about him?
   c. What did the biggest wolf plan to do? What did he learn?
   d. What were the two plans? Why did each one fail?
   e. What happened to the wolf each time he smelled Mucky?
   f. Can you think of a way the wolf could have been successful?

2. Below are incidents that occurred in the story. Ask the students to tell what happened after each of the following events:
   a. The flies buzzed around the moose's head.
   b. Mucky walked through the forest.
   c. The biggest wolf was hungry.
   d. The wind changed directions.
   e. Mucky couldn't understand what the wolf was saying.
   f. The wolf took off the gas mask.
   g. The wolf left the forest.

Activities to Try

1. Have students select episodes from the story to retell in their own words.

2. Divide the class into groups of three. They may reread the story taking the parts of Mucky, the wolf or the narrator.

3. The following activities will help the group create dialogue for a play. Read the following situations to them. How well can they recall what Mucky and the wolf said to each other?

   a. What did Mucky say when the wolf told him he was going to eat him?

   b. What did the wolf say with the clothespin on his nose?

   c. What did the moose say to the wolf wearing a gas mask?

   d. What did the wolf say after he removed the gas mask?

   In the following circumstances,

   a. What might Mucky have said when the animals avoided him?

   b. What could the skunks have said when Mucky walked by them?

   c. What might the wolves have said when they heard the biggest wolf's plan?

   d. What could the wolf have said when he left the forest?

   e. What might the flies, birds and frogs have said when they saw Mucky coming?

4. Prepare and present a puppet show to retell the story. Use stick puppets. Several different colored wolves will be needed—gray, yellow, green and purple. Help the students write lines to add to the original dialogue by author Jonathan Allen. Direct the class artists to paint backdrops for the changing of scenery.

Follow-Up Activities

Moose and Wolves

Give the students opportunities to read, look at pictures and view films about moose and wolves. Have them report their findings. They may work individually or collaborate in small groups to produce a book about one of the animals. They should write one fact on each page and include pictures from magazines or student-drawn illustrations.

Animals and Smell

Animals are more dependent than humans on their sense of smell. Salmon use their smell to return to their place of birth. Bees, hunting nectar, locate flowers by detecting their fragrance. Birds living along the ocean can smell clams buried below the sand. Most other birds have no sense of smell and depend on their keen eyes and ears to find food.

Discover how other animals use their sense of smell.

94   Smell

How Fast Do Odors Travel?

Demonstrate how molecules travel through the air unseen. Pour vinegar in a saucer and place in the center of the room. Have students close their eyes and raise their hands when they smell the vinegar.

Let half the class observe the other half as different substances are tested. Notice the time it takes for the odor to travel to the farthest students.

Smell/Taste Zone

Smell/Taste Connection

To demonstrate how our sense of smell aids our ability to taste, set up a tasting center where a few children at a time may participate. For each person you will need three flavors of fruit juice, three small paper cups and a blindfold.

Have each child smell and then taste the juices while they are blindfolded. Can they identify each flavor?

When they sample a second time, they should also hold their noses while they are tasting.

The object of this test is not to identify the juice but to experience how the sense of smell aids our ability to taste. Discuss how the flavor is enhanced because we are able to smell it.

How Does It Smell?

Walk around the school campus or the neighborhood. How many different odors can be identified? When the group returns to the classroom, note the various smells. They can be described as floral, spicy, fruity, forest-like or other. Let the students categorize the smells.

As a variation, proceed as above, but walk with a partner taking turns wearing a blindfold. Can they tell where they are by the smell? Can they identify the smell?

☐ It Smells Like . . .

A variety of scratch and stiff stickers will provide opportunities to detect different odors.

1. Prepare a set of "smell" cards. Place a sticker on each index card. Have students identify the smell without looking. They may also sort them, grouping similar smells.

2. Prepare pairs of cards with identical stickers. Blindfolded students take turns matching the cards.

Suggested Activities

Mmmmm or Yuck?

There are smells that everyone likes and odors that no one cares for. No group agrees on everything.

1. Survey the class to discover likes and dislikes. What are some smells they like to sniff? What are some smells they don't like?

2. Make a chart to record the results of the survey. Add a third column for the undecided.

3. Discover why some aromas are pleasant and others are not. Ask why they think the same odor is liked by some and disliked by others.

Smells from A to Z

Compile a class alphabet book of smells. Assign each class member a letter of the alphabet or give each group a few letters. They may use rubber stamps, computer graphics or draw their own pictures. Have them write a sentence to describe the aroma.

Sample: The smelly skunk made me hold my nose.

Smell Collage

A visit to the spice rack will provide materials for an aromatic piece of art that is colorful, too.

Materials

Materials
ground cinnamon
cloves
ginger
paprika
curry
pepper
sample of whole spices if available
diluted white glue
brushes
tagboard
pencils

Directions

1. Set up work areas, one for each spice, so the surplus may be recycled.

2. Give a 5" x 5" (13 x 13 cm) square of tagboard to each student.

3. Direct them to draw an irregular shape using most of the surface. Then add lines to divide the shape into five or six sections.

4. The students rotate from center to center where they apply glue and sprinkle on the spices.

5. While the glue is drying, let them examine the whole spices and talk about how they are used in cooking.

6. Direct them to tap off the excess and move on to the next station.

Scratch and Sniff

Enhance a writing experience with an assortment of scratch and sniff stickers.

1. Introduce rebus writing to the group. Describe how pictures and writing are combined to convey a message. Assign a picture writing activity using the stickers.

2. Select one sticker to feature in a story or weave a tale using more than one. Demonstrate, adapting the students suggestions to complete a brief story incorporating the sense of smell. After selecting stickers, have the students compose their own story.

Resources

Nonfiction

Parker, Steve. *Touch, Taste, and Smell.* London: Franklin Watts, 1989.

Ruis, Maria, J.M. Parramon, and J.J. Puig. *The Five Senses: Smell.* Hauppauge, New York: Barron's, 1985.

Silverstein, Alvin, Virginia and Robert. *Smell, the Subtle Sense.* New York: Morrow Junior Books, 1992.

Fiction

Allen, Jonathan. *Mucky Moose.* New York: Macmillan Publishing Company, 1990.

Clip Art for Smell

olfactory
nerves

nasal
passage

nostril

Clip Art for Smell

The Five Senses

Putting It All Together

Introduce to the class one or more of the following activities that sum up the five senses.

Can You?

1. Read the poem below and discuss.

> Can you smell a rainbow?
> Can you touch a star?
>
> Can you see an echo
> Coming from afar?
>
> Can you see the sunset?
> Can you hear the rain?
> Can you touch a snowflake
> On a windowpane?
>
> Can you hear a moonbeam?
> Can you taste the sky?
> Can you touch a planet
> Spinning swiftly by?
>
> Can you taste an apple?
> Can you smell the sea?
> Can you hear a robin
> Singing in the tree?
>
>   by Patricia O'Brien

2. Answer the following questions:

   a. What does a sunset look like?

   b. What does an apple taste like?

   c. If you could smell a rainbow, what would it smell like?

   d. How does a moonbeam sound?

   e. What does a planet feel like?

3. Without being concerned with rhyme, have the students create some mixed-up sense lines of their own.

Me Cube

Materials

cube patterns on tagboard
(see page 22), one for
each student
scissors
felt-tipped pens
crayons
pencil
glue

Directions Each side of the cube will feature one of the senses. The sixth side is for the student's name. They may include favorite sights, sounds, smells, tastes and things to feel; information about each sense organ; riddles; poems or any sense-related material. The artwork should be completed before assembling the cubes.

sight

smell

taste

hear

touch

meow

Categories

Copy and distribute the worksheet on page 110. Discuss the sample of sense impressions at the beach. Select other places to explore and work together to discover how senses add to our enjoyment.

Glossary

Compile a glossary of terms related to the senses. Refer to the "Words to Know" boxes in each section. They may include other terms that come to mind. Some of the entries may be illustrated.

102 The Five Senses

Poster

Divide the class into five groups. Each group is responsible for a poster featuring one of the senses. Suggestions are mentioned below.

1. Create an acrostic. Arrange the letters of the key word vertically. Use each letter to begin a word or phrase that describes the featured sense.

2. Write an eye-catching slogan.

3. Complete: Because we have eyes we can see _____.

Sense Collage

Create a collage, a collection of words and pictures that have to do with one topic or idea. Feature the five senses or focus on one. Search through magazines for appropriate words and pictures that convey the theme. Arrange them creatively and glue in place.

Picture Study

Collect several pictures that will stimulate creative expression. Display one picture at a time and discuss what it would be like if they were in the scene. To extend the activity, provide a variety of pictures from which the students may choose. They may select an idea from below to write or dictate.

1. Write titles for the pictures.

2. Create a story featuring one of the senses.

3. Write a factual account explaining how the senses enhance our appreciation of a place.

Picture This

To summarize an outing or a holiday celebration, instruct the students to draw a scene that includes things to see, taste, touch, hear and smell. They may later exchange their papers with a partner who will try to identify the various sensations featured in the picture.

Popcorn: A Sensible Snack

Popcorn can be experienced by all the senses. Ask the students to tell why they think popcorn pops? List their answers. How many different responses can they give?

1. Read aloud and talk about all or part of *The Popcorn Book*, by Tomie de Paola.

2. Spread newspaper out on the floor. Place an electric popper without a lid in the center. Before turning it on, ask the students to predict what they think will happen. Ask them to guess how far the popped corn will travel?

   Note: Pretest the popper to see how far back the children should be seated.

3. Read and enjoy *The Popcorn Dragon*, by Jane Thayer.

Things to Do with Popcorn

Weigh it. How much do the kernels weigh before they are popped? After?

Watch it. How do the kernels react to the heat?

Listen to it. How long did it take before you heard it begin to pop? Describe the sound.

Smell it. When did you start to smell it?

Measure it. How far did the farthest kernels travel?

String it. What animals would enjoy a special treat?

Glue it. Can you think of an art project where you can use popcorn?

Popcorn Art

Use air-popped corn to make a springtime tree. Have the students draw a tree trunk with spreading branches. Then glue the popcorn onto the limbs.

Sense Poem

While the popcorn is popping, brainstorm ideas for a sense poem. List all contributions under the appropriate headings. (Looks like . . . , Sounds like . . . , etc.) After enjoying a popcorn snack, have each student pick favorite phrases to include in their poems.

Popcorn

Looks like _____.

Sounds like _____.

Smells like _____.

Feels like _____.

Tastes like _____.

As a follow up, copy and distribute page 111 to the students. They may select any topic to explore with their senses, write their ideas and compose a sense poem.

Resources

Nonfiction

Aliki. *My Five Senses*. New York: Crowell, 1989.

Ardley, Neil. *The Science Book of Senses*. San Diego: Gulliver Books, 1992.

Cole, Joanna. *You Can't Smell with Your Ear*. New York: Grosset & Dunlap, 1994.

Gaskin, John. *The Senses*. New York: Franklin Watts, 1985.

Martin, Paul D. *Messengers to the Brain*. Washington, D.C.: National Geographic Society, 1984.

Miller, Margaret. *My Five Senses*. New York: Simon & Schuster, 1994.

Fiction

De Paola, Tomie. *The Popcorn Book*. New York: Holiday House, 1978.

Thayer, Jane. *The Popcorn Dragon*. New York: Morrow Junior Books, 1989.

Name _____

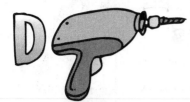 Categories

Choose any five letters. Write one at the top of each column. Fill in the spaces below with names of things you can see, hear, touch, taste or smell. Each word should start with the letter at the top of the column.

See					
Hear					
Touch					
Taste					
Smell					

I Use My Senses

In each box of the chart, write the name of a place you could visit. Think of how your senses help you to enjoy the spot. An example has been done for you.

Place	👁	👂	👃	✋	👄
beach	sparkling waves	squawking gulls	salty air	grilled hot dogs	hot sand

Name _____

 **Sense Poem**

Pick a topic. Think about how it appeals to each of the senses. Write your ideas in each column.

_____
topic

Looks like . . .   **Sounds like . . .**   **Smells like . . .**

_____   _____   _____

_____   _____   _____

_____   _____   _____

_____   _____   _____

Tastes like . . .   **Feels like . . .**

_____   _____

_____   _____

_____   _____

_____   _____

Select one phrase from each section to complete each line of the poem. Write and illustrate your poem on a separate sheet of paper.

Clip Art for the Five Senses

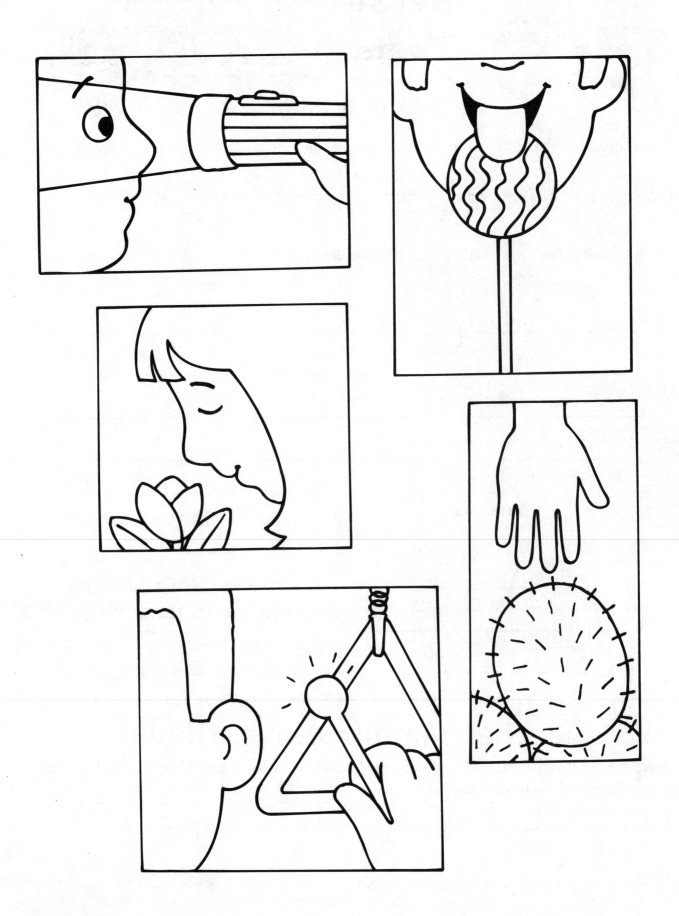